Reviews

"Insightful; on the mark writing. Pattimari has a vast grasp of the human psyche, its frailties and strengths. I recommend it to all who want to understand the human condition better."
Graham Diamond, author of *Forest Wars*, *The Thief of Kalimar*, and numerous other novels.

"A book well-written; filled with marvelous power"
Charles Hass, MD, Internal Medicine

"As a practicing Clinical Psychologist I feel that this is an important book for people to read and integrate into their lives. The concepts presented in this book such as positive thinking, how the mind works and how something negative can be turned into a positive in your life are so relevant to helping solve the problems people are facing today and will help with relationships and being happy. The Stories and poems will also help the reader remember the concepts being presented. Too many self help books make psychology too hard to understand; confusing, and hard to remember. I want to commend these authors for choosing to write this book about this very relevant material that will help the reader with the problems of today in an easy to read format that can be understood to make life better."

Ronald G. Huston, PhD, MSW, MPH
Licensed Clinical Psychologist

"Powerful book; Pattimari has always impressed me with her insight into the psychological world. A must to read!"
Jeanne Trachman, One to One Magazine

"This is such a fascinating book on how we can change our life with positive thinking and with mind power. I think reading this will be helpful for anyone. It would certainly be an asset to any person's bookshelf. This could help one turn their life around in a positive way. Stamping out all the negative thoughts, and replace them with happy positive ones. This book would be such a great gift for the special people in our lives. I have read other books that Pattimari has written, and she is a great author, and I have enjoyed them all. I salute Pattimari and her friends for a job well done!"
Sara Brannon, writer, New Orleans

"This book has many helpful ideas for anyone to use in their personal lives. I'm glad that I had the opportunity to add my personal story to the book. I thank the authors for writing such a good reference book.
Readers: Positive thinking will change your life if you integrate it in your daily thoughts."
Linda Huston, M.A., C.F.L.E. (Certified Family Life Educator)

Sometimes Your Greatest Misery Can Be Your Greatest Happiness

By

Pattimari Sheets-Diamond
Stories and quotes by JoAnn Kite
Charlotte Huston-Johnson

Lulu Publishing

PMSD

Sometimes Your Greatest Misery can be Your Greatest Happiness

Copyright © 2010 by Pattimari Sheets-Diamond

The information in this book is intended to be educational and helpful not for diagnosis or treatment of any kind.

ISBN 978-0-557-42633-1

For more information for bulk purchases, please contact Pattimari Sheets-Diamond at: pattimari@hotmail.com

Procrastination is like a credit card: it's a lot of fun until you get the bill.

Christopher Parker

Lulu Publishing 2010

Contents

Chapter One
Understanding How Your Mind Works

Chapter Two
Our Expectations can Cause us Pain

Chapter Three
Our Thoughts Make Things Happen

Chapter Four
Our Unconscious Mind

Chapter Five
Our Health and Information

Chapter Six
Quotes and Poems to Think About

Chapter Seven
Why do we stay in Abusive Relationships?

Chapter Eight
Change Your State of Mind

Chapter Nine
The Power of the Mind

Chapter Ten
More Poems and quotes

Chapter Eleven
Stories of Value

Chapter Twelve
How Meditation Makes your Mind Clearer

Chapter Thirteen
Our Thoughts

Chapter Fourteen
Helpful Hints for Treasure Hunting and Short Stories

Chapter Fifteen
Books read with inspiration

Chapter Sixteen
JoAnn's Soul Food for Depression

Chapter Seventeen
Charlotte's Story of Changing our Thoughts

Chapter Eighteen
A Women's Group Story and More

Lulu publishing

About the Author

Pattimari Sheets-Diamond's field is Psychology; she has worked with Autistic and ADHD children, family counseling, women' groups and workshops. Her thrill is writing, her joy is gardening and traveling. She feels her greatest gift to the world is to help people smile and to live life in a positive way where they can attract good things into their life. She resides in California where she lives her life to its fullest. Pattimari1675@hotmail.com

****

JoAnn Kite has been studying Jungian psychology for over 30 years, and is interested in all psycho/spiritual traditions, knowing that at the core of each there is *Truth* to guide our hearts and minds into peace and happiness. She feels a deep connection with *Nature,* especially her mountains and forests. She loves to hike mountain trails around her home. Oneness of the *Earth* and of all humanity is her vision, word and song.

Charlotte Huston-Johnson has written two books, a song and resides in California where she fills up her life with positive thought. She is an angel; always helping others.

P

Lulu publishing

Books Written by Pattimari

Sometimes your Greatest Misery can be your Greatest
Happiness
Time Heals, Forgiveness Mends
Lydia Between Two Worlds
Different Styles of Poetry
Children's Short Stories for all Ages
(look for my next book; Valley of the Sacred Golden Eggs)

Publications by JoAnn Kite

Sometimes your Greatest Misery can be your Greatest
Happiness
Editor's Choice, International Library of Poetry
Poetry published in Arcadia Poetry Press

Books Written byCharlotte Huston-Johnson

Sometimes your Greatest Misery can be your Greatest
Happiness
Lydia Between Two Worlds
Children's Short Stories for all Ages

*Dedicated to all those who
entered my life and brought
new experiences and left
behind love, light and magnificent sunshine.
Also to those who brought
gifts that weren't always what I
expected, but added to my life.*

Pattimari

Dedicated to the One in all of us

Who always turns our misery into happiness.

JoAnn

Dedicated to the world

Charlotte

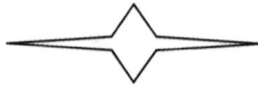

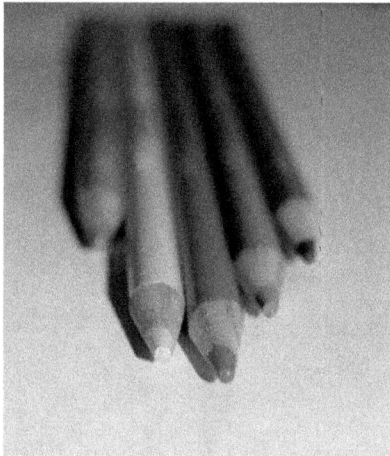

Sometimes your Greatest Misery can be your Greatest Happiness

Foreword

Several months ago, my life buckled out from under me sending me off into the depths of pain like I had never experienced before.

One early morning on August 1, 2009, my husband asked for a divorce and left. Out of my God awful misery came the greatest gift I had ever been given. But I didn't know it until several weeks later.

For three days, I couldn't eat or sleep. I paced. I couldn't cry, nor was I able to see anyone. I felt as if my world had tumbled down into pieces of pain. It was the oddest experience I had ever felt because my mind was fine, but my body went into shock.

A few weeks later, I woke up with a glow in my heart and a smile on my face. Things began happening in my life that made me realize I had been given a wonderful gift.

The freedom that I experienced was filled with amazing new discoveries. People were entering my life like I had never experienced before. I got offers to participate in groups, programs, books, seminars and discussions that filled my soul and spirit with love and made me happier than I had ever been in my entire life.

This book is about how to make your life better by your own thoughts. I truly believe our thoughts control what happens in our life. I am writing this book to open doors for you to see that you make your own happiness.

As you read each page you will learn how you can have gladness in your life, even when it comes crashing down on you. I had often been told in my life that your greatest misery is where you find your greatest happiness. This book has been written to show you that this is a true statement. I brought in two friends; JoAnn Kite and Charlotte Huston-Johnson to write stories and poems because they are of like mind and over the years we've shared conversations on the power of *thought*. For years we've thought about writing a book; this book has become our reality. JoAnn is not only a scholar when it comes to books and writing, she is my dear friend. Charlotte, I've known for over twenty years and we've been friends since. Her creativity is the best I've encountered. She is a free spirit who has a warm and loving spirit that has always impressed me. She has great insight in the power of thought; experienced it and lives it.

Pattimari

pattimari in touch with nature

Chapter One
Understanding How Your Mind Works

Let's begin with the word *ANGER*. There are degrees of anger. Hate, Fury and Rage? Yes, but let's go further and talk about words you may not have affiliated with anger. Words like; annoyance, irritation, frustration, disturbance, disgusted, hurt, mad, hostile, livid, hate and the list goes on.

Perhaps a story about annoyance will help give you a clear picture of how it's associated with anger. It might allow you to see there are different forms of anger; those you might not have thought about.

☼ Story 1

One morning Carolyn jerked awake and realized her alarm hadn't gone off. "Late another day," she moaned. Yes, she was late again getting to work. (1st annoyance) After she arrived at work, her boss told her if she was late again, she'd be fired. (2nd annoyance) She poured a cup of coffee and accidentally spilled it all over her new dress. Through-out the day she had a few more annoyances and by late afternoon she was angry. She began snapping at anyone who got in her way.

Hurt is another word most people might not connect with anger. But *hurt* can become anger. In fact, it is a deep wounding type of anger. Usually we want the person that hurt us to feel pain and hurt too, so we strike out to get even or become vindictive.

Little *irritations* can become full blown anger. They get to a steaming point where divorce can occur or where we turn away from our best friends. A wise friend of mine once told me about an old Chinese proverb: The more you push a feeling down, the bigger it gets.

Disappointment is a big source of anger. *Powerlessness* produces anger. Being *controlled, pressures, confusion boredom, death, separation or divorce* are all forms of losses which can create anger. *Sarcasm, embarrassment, shame and rejection* can lead to anger.

Anger comes from many different places and when we're aware of all the words that cause anger, we can understand a little better how our mind works.

With more understanding, we then know how to deal with our anger before it soars out of control.

The first thing we need to learn is to **not** hold our emotions in, but allow them to come out as we feel them and deal with them before they get to a steaming point where we are out of control.

Anger is a *normal emotion* and there is nothing wrong with feeling anger. We have a right to be angry about things in our life, but again, if we hold our anger in, it builds up to a steaming point where it soars out of control and we are no longer in charge of our emotions.

☼ Story 2

It was an important night for Cecil because he was going to receive a special certificate for being the best employee of the month. His friend, Rudy, had agreed to pick him up since his wife was using their car. The ceremony was to be at 7 o'clock that night and Rudy was picking Cecil up at 6:30pm. Cecil was dressed and waiting for his friend, but by 6:45pm, Rudy hadn't shown up yet so he began to worry. He called Rudy, but he didn't answer his phone. By 7pm Cecil called a taxi and didn't get to the ceremony until 7:30pm. People were waiting and his boss was quite disappointed in Cecil.

Later that night, Rudy dropped by and apologized for forgetting to pick Cecil up. Cecil said, "Oh, that's okay" and let Rudy off the hook. But later, he began snapping at his wife and the more he thought about Rudy, the angrier he became, until he got to a steaming point and ended up feeling *resentment* toward Rudy. His resentment turned into *depression* and before Cecil realized it, he had acquired *bitterness*.

Cecil had a right to be angry at Rudy and to tell him that he had let him down. If he had, his anger wouldn't have soared to a steaming level where he not only took it out on others, but caused himself a mixture of feelings; resentment, bitterness and depression.

When we tuck and stuff our natural emotions it does damage to us. It grows until it reaches levels that are out of control.

Charlotte & Pattimari

Toasting to life

The Healer Within

Down to the murky depths again
Heart pounding in the night
Back where the anger churns so thick
Where I can't see the Light.
Down, on down I fall again
Where chains and weakness loom.
I brace myself and grit my teeth
in fast-descending gloom.
And yet - I realize it now!
I've faced this pit before
Where all seems sad and hopeless
With the shouts of inner war
And so I stand now calmly
With my face turned toward the Light
Knowing that this misperception
Never wins the fight!
I've gone this road so many times
In my tormented past
I let the anger take control

And win the fight at last,

But now I'm looking deep within

To that calm and centered One

My Higher Self - where all is peace

And angry thoughts are gone.

© JoAnn Kite, 2010

Quotes

There are only two ways to live your life. One is as though nothing is a miracle. The other is as though everything is a miracle."
Albert Einstein

The final forming of a person's character lies in their own hands.
Anne Frank

We are continually engaged in the evolution of self and world – and we have the power to choose, moment by moment, between that which gives life and that which deals death.
Parker J. Palmer

One need remain in hell no longer than one chooses to; we can rise to any heaven we ourselves choose; and when we choose so to rise, all the higher powers of the Universe combine to help us heavenward. R. W. Trine

We get in life that which we focus on. Continual focus on darkness leads us, as individuals and as a society, further into darkness. Focus on the light brings us into the light.
Marianne Williamson

Daffodil Dark Night

Yesterday, the daffodils in my garden were budding with the promise of splendor in the early spring sun. Today they are buried deep under a foot of freshly fallen snow which is still falling, no end in sight. The birds are silent, huddled together for warmth on the leafing branches. The sky and the landscape are covered in white whirling veils, shot through with silence and mystery, like Isis shrouded as she descends to the underworld; nothing moves, nothing stirs, nothing sounds.

What must my daffodils be 'thinking', I wonder. They have grown about a quarter of an inch in the last few days, and up until yesterday they were happily greening themselves in the sun, being serenaded with sparrow song and danced by the passing breezes. Now they are in total darkness and will be for quite some time, unless mild weather comes quickly. Do they feel abused by nature? Do they cry for the lost sunshine and their freedom to enjoy it? Do they feel threatened by these 'dark' forces that apparently do not have their best interests at heart?

Perhaps they do. Responsive Intelligence is everywhere, even in plants; and in whatever nameless Way daffodils respond to their environment, their yesterday with sunshine had a much different feeling than their frozen today has. For them, today must feel like they are being strangled in a cold blanket of death. So I send them thoughts of love and encouragement, knowing that they will survive their dark night, as all of us will, no matter what the circumstances.

Precious daffodil darlings, this must be a very trying time for you, you have lost all sensual signals of life. Perhaps you feel abandoned in the white, hollow void, as though all around is meaningless and chaotic, far from the freedom and warmth of sunshine, air and bird song. Take courage, blossoms-to-be! This time is not the chaos it seems to you. It is not counter-productive to your best interests; not evil in any way! Your senses may tell you differently, your environment may scream bondage and misery, but this is only so that you may be chiseled more perfectly into who you are meant to Become. Look past your senses, dear sprouts….look behind your senses, within, to the root from which your floweriness, and all life, is ultimately drawn. There you will inbreathe the essence of your nature, and it will manifest the true Daffodil through you, the Infinite energy that shapes everything into fulfillment for all time.

What seems desolate is really germination and gestation; what seems horrible, unfair and unbearable is really an opportunity to come forth to new awakening. And what seems to be death is really a glorious birth chamber wherein we ever become more of who we are truly meant to be.

In the meantime, be still, dear daffodils, and dear everyone. Be still and *know* that all is well, and all is very well, and will be forever so.

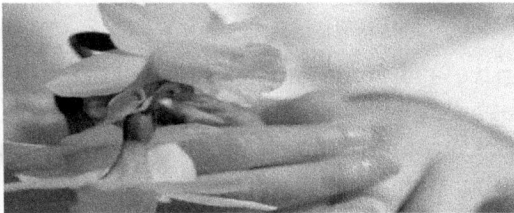

JoAnn

Golden Nuggets

It is late summer in the forest, all golden and rust and orange, and fully ripe with fruits and nuts, I wander along the tiny mountain path, gathering fresh raspberries as I go, musing on the wonder of a forest that transforms itself in only a few months from a bundle of dry sticks to the lushness of wild lilac and juicy purple raspberries. It's a day for quiet reflection in this late summer sun. The ferns on the edge of the trail tickle my ankles as I make my way to one of my favorite spots under an old fir tree.

At last I arrive and settle down on a rock with a spectacular view of the valley below. Everything is so full and lush, with fat, lazy bees buzzing from flower to flower, and the cicadas are singing their humming hymn in the treetops. Suddenly, out of the corner of my eye I see a little red squirrel jump up out of the brush to my right, landing on a small log not far from where I'm sitting.

Such a precious little creature! With her bushy red tail and perky little tufted ears, she looks like a tiny elf of the forest, always ready for a treasure hunt or a quick sprint up a tree. Now she seems particularly bright-eyed and bushy-tailed as she reaches down under the log and brings up a large, meaty nut, cracking the shell with her strong little teeth.

She sits there in a calm and meditative way, quietly munching her nut and gazing out across the vista below. From side to side she glances, focusing now on the occasional bird gliding along below, or raising her eyes to take in the sweep of the hills in the soft, late summer sunshine. How privileged I feel to be sitting here, almost beside her, sharing with her the beauty and bounty of the forest!

As winter approaches and the days grow shorter, there will be red and gray squirrels running throughout the forest, busily gathering themselves a cache of nuts for the winter, stuffing their cheeks with them until they look like funny, furry little blowfish. They'll spend their winters snug and dry under the snows in their little dens, with plenty of nuts in their 'cupboards' to keep them well and healthy until Spring breaks across the landscape once again. Their natural instincts work perfectly for them, providing everything they need to live healthy, happy lives.

And now, as I gaze at this sweet creature before me, she reminds me how we humans, too, ought to prepare for the winter times of our lives - not only for the physical winter, but for those winters of the heart, when all seems dry as sticks in the wind and the light is dim, giving us no direction, no warmth, as barren as a frozen winter landscape. What 'nuggets' should we gather to keep us from the famine of these dark winter nights of our being?

The golden nuggets for our nourishment live deep within the dens of our inner being, and they are there for us to 'munch' anytime we please. Hope, joy, inner sunshine, laughter - these were all encoded within us, just as the squirrel is encoded to find what she needs in time of want. Open your heart to feel the wonder and joy of Life deep inside your being, and before you know it, you will be protected and guided through your long winter night, into a spring time that warms and cheers and heals you.

Red Squirrel has finished eating and is meticulously cleaning herself with her tiny furry hands. She gives one last glance to the sky and the hills and then jumps like a little acrobat off her log and then turns and notices me with a flick of her tail and some startled chatter. I smile back at her and we gaze for a timeless moment into each other's eyes, the civilized human being and the wild creature of the forest. As she scampers away into the woods, I can't help but think how much alike we are in our creature hood, each of us dependent on the 'nuggets' which *life* has given us to sustain us and see us through our lives. Surely, the *life* which provides for the needs of these tiny little animals can also be trusted to provide for us human beings!

The spider's web, the beaver's dam, the bird's nest are all purposeful. The way the leaves of a tree are designed is extraordinarily fitting: their shape permits them to intercept light, the source of energy for photosynthesis, as well as gas and heat exchange with the air. Again, every animate form has the propensity and the astonishing ability to fulfill itself, to consummate itself, and, when necessary, ingeniously to circumvent obstacles in its way. In short, intelligence and purpose are evident throughout nature. Anna F Lemkow

JoAnn's Safe in the Storm

It was a good day for quiet musing. The sun was warm and the birds were soaring through the trees singing their lighthearted songs, as I sat back against an old log on the forest floor. Squirrels and chipmunks scurried about in innocent delight and bright butterflies brought bursts of brilliant color as they flitted through the wooded landscape.

I'm not sure how long I sat there under the old fir tree. The mountain forest wove its spell on me before I knew it, and my thoughts and reflections gave way to a peaceful, dreaming doze, when all of a sudden a sound like angry dragons ripped into my awareness and I woke up to see the sky dark with rumbling warnings of an approaching storm. I hastily gather up my belongings, fearing the worst as I see lightning slash between the trees on the horizon, and the woodland becomes strangely silent as all the little creatures scurry off to the shelter of their dens and nests. Angry and disgusted with the sudden change in weather, all my peaceful musings have apparently disappeared in the dark clouds.

The wind picks up, tossing branches about in the thickening darkness as I quickly mount my bicycle and make a hurried run out of the forest toward home. My heart pounds, my skin gets clammy, my throat tight and parched, and I feel the primal fear and anger rise up in me as two more slashes of lightning rip through the darkening sky. Gone, for the moment, are all thoughts of peace, all lazy musings on the joy of this day. All my senses are gripped by fear as I pedal my bike as fast as I can, praying that I'll make it home before the storm unleashes its untamed fury. Yet even in the face of apparent disaster, my inner self is assuring me that even this very frightening experience is somehow a necessary part of the seasons of my life. I take a deep breath and continue riding into the storm.

One of the wonderful things about all of us is that we have the power to choose how we will respond to our experiences. Even in the worst storms of our lives, there is pure Gold awaiting our discovery in the depths of our being.

Fear and anger aren't all that I'm experiencing, I realize, as I look closely into myself. Deeper than the fear and anger, more real than the raging storm, lies the inner Sun that always lights our way. And this inner Sun is here with me now, whispering for me to have faith in Life, no matter what the outer circumstances, urging me to be brave in the shining within our hearts, and we can bask in this pure Sunshine at all times, if we choose to do so.

Storms will come and go in our life; of this we can be sure. But at the same time, even in the midst of the storm's angry tossing, we can still choose to relax in the inner Sunshine which tells us that somehow all things do work toward good for us and for all. Implanted within us is the unfailing capacity to find the good which is in every situation. We have the ability and the power to transmute the storms into a calm awareness by seeing the Sun shining always behind the dark thunder clouds of anger and fear.

Breathlessly, I ride my bike down the mountain, hair flying free as the first raindrops sting my face. By the time I make it to my warm and safe home, I'm soaked to the skin yet energized by the dancing electricity of the storm, and I come inside with a deep sense of gratefulness and joy in being alive. How fortunate I am, I think, as I towel-dry my hair, change out of my soggy clothing, and fix myself a hot cup of coffee. No matter what the day brings, I know I've been given the ability to see the Sun shining pure Gold in my heart, even in the worst of storms....and so can you. See the Sunshine always beaming within you, the Light which is your constant inner peace and joy, no matter how furious the storms rage around you, and you'll make it Home safely too.

———◇———

Back on Back

Back to the first beginnings,
To the Earthy solid core
To the innermost and deepest point
Where anger is no more
Back where the Sun shines constantly
I make my spiral way
Where 'happily ever after' lives
Forever and a day
Back to the first beginnings,
To the glowing inner hearth
Where butterflies and singing birds
Are flying in my heart
Back to my own integrity,
Where I so truly find
That the core of my own
Being is a peaceful heart and mind.
JoAnn Kite © 2010

Fill It Up

When your cup is empty,
and your heart is low;
fill it up
with happy thoughts.
Open doors
back to light and song.

Pattimari © 2010

Spirit

S is for soul of life and energy

P is for the power it gives

I is for the intent of the true feeling

R is for regarding a state of mind

I is for infused with fun loving

T is for truth and state of mind

Char Johnson , 2008

Friend

F Friend is hard to find

R Reaches for your hand

I I'm so glad we are friends

E Eternal, forever friends

N Needing friendship never stops

D Devine friends are hard to find

Charlotte Johnson, copyright 2008

In the Darkness of the Night

All through the night,
in the darkened room
was blight.
Setting near the edge,
you could see the light.
Low singing came to my delight
A song filled my heart,
and everything was all right.

Pattimari

The Rising Dawn

Whenever it seems that

Life's bright dreams

Are trampled in the mire;

When hope falls low

And all is so

Damned bleak,

Without desire,

Be sure that this black shroud of mist

Will someday disappear

This night of woe in depths below

Will rise in Morning clear,

The fertile soil of tears and toil

Will germinate the Light

And bring you forth

To glorious Birth

With victory and might. There is no Life

Without the strife,

But woes aren't what they seem;

Be still, you must!

Now wait in Trust -

The Night will Birth

New Dreams.

JoAnn Kite

Chapter Two

Our Expectations can Cause us Pain

We all have *expectations* on how it should turn out, or how he or she should be or feel. We've been conditioned to have certain value systems and when others get outside of our value system, we become critical. In some cases we become angry or disappointed in them.

The first thing that is important to learn is what a colleague once said to me. He said, 'What I say about you says nothing about you, it only says something about me.' Another colleague once told me that a friend had misled him. His friend told him it was an excellent movie and he should go see it. He did. He came back feeling misled. What he later learned was his friend might not have misled him at all because there was a possibility that he thought it was an excellent movie. You see, what someone else thinks is good, may not be good for you. That's what makes the world go around, we are all different in our own ways and when we realize this, we become less critical of others.

We're back to the thought: What I say about you says nothing about you it only says something about me.

Life cannot be lived on untrue premises or filled with deluded behavior without creating pressure sooner or later even though it be felt only in the haunting fears or vicious nightmares of one's dreams.
Fritz Kunkel, psychiatrist

It all depends on how we look at things, and not on how they are in themselves. The least of things with meaning is worth more in life than the greatest of things without it. Carl Jung

Peaceful states of mind, that is, moods without conflict, serene, deliberate, and well-balanced, so far as they are lasting, depend on specially well-developed attitudes.
Carl Jung

Most folks are about as happy as they make up their minds to be.
Abraham Lincoln, 16th American President

One person sincerely practicing goodwill in a family can completely change its attitudes. As a man thinks, hopes and wills so is he. This is a statement of an immutable fact.
Alice A. Bailey

The Way It Is

No matter how dark the doubting
Or the anger seems to be,
It's really just a game we play -
In Truth, we are quite free.
No matter how sad the parting
Or the tides of fortune seem
It's really just a dance within
This One eternal dream
No matter how deep the sorrow
Or the pain of Life might be
We triumph over everything -
In Truth we are quite free
JoAnn Kite
©2004

Be Still

Be still!

What are you feeling right now?

Harness your feelings,

Make them what

You wish to feel

This moment

Right now!

Pattimari, 2010

You can move your thoughts to what you desire - right now. Change the pattern to happy thoughts because when you do, happy thoughts will come and happenings in your life move to the upbeat.

Realize when you are in a negative frame of mind, you attract negative energies to enter your life.

Negative reactions attract more of the same.

If you find it difficult, slow your mind down. How do you do that? Meditate. Start with 5 minutes a day.

Chapter Three

Our Thoughts Make Things Happen

Last month a colleague of mine said, when a person is a reactor he doesn't have control of his life. He continued to say, if you're really interested in taking charge of your life, then it's important to understand the connection between your thoughts, feelings and behavior.

In the process of learning to take control of your life, it is important to shift from giving your power away to others to recognizing your own thoughts and feelings.

Many times decisions are based on what others will think about you or what has happened in your past. You know that dark side that you don't want anyone to know about. It's stuffed away so deeply that we don't even remember it many times, but nonetheless, we react from those feelings. Those unconscious pictures can affect our actions, our thoughts and behavior. You may not understand what caused you to react to a certain incident because it has been stuffed away where it isn't noticed. But we do know we reacted and it didn't feel good or it didn't make sense to us at the time.

Being out of touch with your thoughts only causes you to make bad decisions. So let's talk about how you can get in touch with your thoughts, your feelings and change the behavior you're now experiencing that causes you great pain.

First of all, realize we all have a dark past. Yes, we all do! Yes, some are worse than others, but nonetheless, we all have been hurt or treated poorly sometime in our past, so those happenings have caused us to have dark thoughts or to become critical of others. We started reacting instead of truly feeling what we felt at a moment of an incident. Our past will never go away. It is there forever, however, we *can* change our thoughts. We can begin to look at things from a different perspective rather than a negative one, because a negative mind only catches the attention of negative things that happen in our life.

We can be happy. We can change our thoughts so that it attracts positive things to happen in our life.

Does it take work? You bet it does. Does a college degree take work? You bet it does. Yes, it takes work to get past the negative things that we attract in our life.

Let's talk about a computer. If we write something in our computer and then see mistakes, what do we do? We write over them. We change them. They are still there somewhere, but they have been corrected and changed so that when we read the new revised version, we only see the corrected version. Okay, then that's how our thoughts work. And when our thoughts become 'corrected' where they are positive thoughts, we attract positive things to come into our life. Good things come to us - Our life changes.

Let me give you an example of what I experienced in my life at the age of eight. I hadn't done my homework the night before and I knew my teacher was going to scold me. What could I do? I decided to tell my mother I wasn't feeling well the next morning. I got up holding my stomach and said, "Mother, my stomach hurts and I feel like I'm going to throw up." My mother felt my head and said, "Honey, you don't have a fever, but get back in bed, you might be coming down with the flu." I did.

By early afternoon, my stomach really did start hurting and a few moments later, I threw up. I realized at that early age, I had created my illness that day by my thoughts of pretending to be sick. From then on, I became aware that our thoughts attract whatever we think in life. Oh, I'd forget it at times and had to relearn it, but it was something I knew. I notice when I'm feeling wonderfully happy and full of life, good things come my way. But let one little thing happen that discourages me and it seems a flow of negativity floods into my life.

For example, my refrigerator broke down one summer and after that incident my thoughts became fearful. I knew I was trying to save for a vacation and the refrigerator took a good portion of it and I began fearing other things might happen. Guess what? It did. From there my thoughts became more fearful and more negative things happened. When I changed my thoughts from fearing, things stopped happening. Trust me, it does work that way. If you doubt this statement, start paying attention to your thoughts and things that happen good and bad in your life and you'll see it is so.

You must feel good about yourself in order to change your thoughts so the first thing that is needed is for you to get your body in shape. When a body is healthy and in good shape our mind works stronger and is clearer.

This is the way it works, if you don't like your body and how it looks, it will cause you to feel negative about yourself. Your thoughts will be centered on how you feel ugly, overweight or low on energy. So the first thing you need to do is change your eating habits and start exercising. At first it might be difficult to get your energy connected to it, but if you're faithful about exercising five minutes a day, before you know it you can do ten minutes until you get up to thirty minutes a day. I guarantee you by the first month if you're faithful with it, you will feel better and have more energy. Start changing your thoughts immediately and look at your body with love and appreciation because if you hate your body, it's going to be that much more difficult to begin your goal of getting your body into shape.

What you put into your body is equally important. Begin by eating more fruits and veggies. Cook them in a way so you'll want more. When I first started I sautéed my veggies with yogurt butter which is one half the fats that butter has. I knew it had to taste good in order for me to get motivated. I cut up all the veggies I loved; onions, sweet potatoes, squash, mushrooms, carrots, cabbage and any other veggie available I liked, then I sautéed them in the yogurt butter and by the second week I had more energy and I begin to really love the dish. We need protein, so I started cutting up chicken and putting it into the dish. I started walking one block a day and the next week, two, then the three week, three blocks. By two months I was walking a mile and loving it. My thoughts were clear and I felt absolutely good about myself. I didn't see the weight change until the third month, but the energy was so powerful that it didn't even disturb me. When I began, I told myself that I was doing it for energy and that's what I got. Before the year was out, I was totally in love with my new look and my energy was soaring. My mind was thinking positive thoughts and I liked myself. My motivation went sky high and before I knew it I was enrolled in college for my degree, which by the way, I didn't feel I could do because I felt I wasn't smart enough. But with A's and B's that first year, I knew my thinking had been wrong. I didn't even waste my time wondering where I got that past thought. I just knew it wasn't correct. I realized that I was smart.

JoAnn's Lessons from an Inchworm

Hiking along the beautiful forest trails near my home usually always makes me happy. Even on gray, rainy days the wonder and beauty of the forest are enough to keep my spirit soaring on wings of peace and happiness, but today, even though the sun was shining brightly, I wasn't soaring at all. I'd just found out that I would have to quit my job, and probably would never be able to work again.

I dearly loved that job. All my friends were there; they seemed to me like a second family, and I was disheartened and very discouraged from having to leave it behind. I was angry, too, thinking; "But it's so unfair! Why do such bad things have to happen to me?"

The breezes were warm today, and all the little birds were happily chirping, but as I made my way up the winding forest trail, I scarcely heard their cheery chatter. I was so wrapped up in thoughts of self-pity that it was difficult to see or hear anything else, even in this lush and beautiful mountain.

I came to a favorite spot, a large, flat rock beneath a white birch tree, and sat down wearily, blinking back tears of pain and frustration. All those years I had put into that job, loving it and doing the best I could, and now this! It was such a painful, abrupt end to one of my biggest joys in life.

I was about to bury my face in my hands and weep my heart out, when I noticed a tiny little inchworm on the forest floor. He didn't look happy there, kept rising up on his tiny little back legs, jerking his head around, trying to sense, I think, which way he should go to find a juicy leaf to feed on. He somehow knew his little life depended on this. Up and over the rocks he went, skirting around dead leaves, avoiding a tiny puddle, taking a few moments to catch his breath and plan his next move. It took him a half hour of scrunching and jerking and looking around, to move only about a foot or so.

At one point, it almost looked like he was ready to give up, sitting still for quite some time, only raising his head now and then. He might have even taken a little nap. But always, always, for the next two solid hours, he would begin again, jerk and twist and turn and writhe his way toward - what? All he *knew,* and he definitely *knew* it; he just *had* to get there!

What determination in this tiny creature no bigger than half a toothpick! He knew his goal, he *knew* how to get there, but here he was stuck on the forest floor, no tree in sight for the next two feet; what were his chances of ever finding fulfillment? And yet he kept inching. He kept trying.

Suddenly he didn't look anymore like just a tiny inchworm to me; he began to look like a kind teacher who had come to tell me that life is worth fighting for. Life is worth all the effort we put into it. Life is good, even when we feel like everything is an obstacle. The life force within this tiny creature refuses to give up, keeps on trying, knows there is a worthy goal, and that he's meant to achieve it, and that, for sure, nothing is going to stop him!

I took a twig and gently urged him onto it. Then I lifted him up to the nearby birch tree, and as soon as he saw it he went – zing! – like a little magnet he sprang from twig to tree trunk. I could feel the joy in his teensy little body! He began climbing that tree with a surety born of healthy instinct, inching his way up, scrunch, jerk, lunge forward, again and again and again, up, up, up, until I couldn't see him anymore and he was lost in the paradise of many leaves to feed on.

You and I, dear people, you and I are one with this little inchworm. One in our determined drive to find that which we instinctively *know* will fulfill us and bring calm, peaceful food to ourselves and to many of our brothers and sisters. We may apparently lose our way sometimes and sometimes we may not have the least inkling as to how to move forward, but yet we move, we inch our way along in this world, sure that our instincts are sound and that we will at last reach our goal. Our precious life force wouldn't have it any other way!

Faith in ourselves, and in life itself, is sure to take us to that green, leafy tree of happiness which we all envision for ourselves and each other. We can trust the life that made inchworms and human beings in such a way that they cannot rest until they achieve their life's purpose and goal.

Little inchworm disappeared from my sight a while ago now, and the sun is casting long shadows over the forest, so it's time to pack up my things and be on my way down the mountain. But as I'm realizing that I have been given a tremendous blessing by that tiny, dear little inchworm. Doors may have closed behind me, and my life might seem to be stuck right now in uncertainty and anxiety about my lost past, but I know I'll be all right as long as I remember that there really will be juicy new green beginnings opening up for me, and for all of us, as we make our way through life's trails and trials. We can count on life to carry us through to where we are meant to be, where we can grow and laugh and flourish and be fulfilled. Little Inchworm told me that with every determined little move he made.

Quotes to think about

What you think is what you are

As above so below

As within so without

What goes around, comes around

What goes up must come down

What you give does come back

What you think comes back to you

What you attract is yours

Be careful of your thoughts

———◇———

We sow our thoughts and we reap our actions.
We sow our actions and we reap our habits.
We sow our habits and we reap our characters;
We sow our characters and we reap our destiny.
Anonymous

Think of all the beauty still left around you and be happy.
Anne Frank
Man in the last resource is that which he thinks; he grows
wicked by thinking evil, but if he thinks only that which is
good, the good fills him entirely.
Arthur E. Waite

The inalienable freedom to choose one's attitude of mind persists, even in a Nazi prison camp.
Laurence J. Bendit

Everything has its wonders, even darkness and silence, and I learn whatever state I may be in, therein to be content. Sometimes, it is true, a sense of isolation enfolds me like a cold mist as I sit alone and wait at life's shut gate. Silence sits immense upon my Soul...but then comes hope with a smile and whispers, 'There is joy in self-forgetfulness.' So I try to make the light in others' eyes my sun, the music in others' ears my symphony, the smile on others' lips my happiness.
Helen Keller

Imagination is like the Sun, the light of which is not tangible, but which can set a house on fire. Imagination leads man's life. If he thinks of fire, he is on fire; if he thinks of war, he will cause war. All depends only upon man's imagination to be Sun, i.e., that he imagines wholly that which he wills.
Paracelsus

Procrastination is like a credit card: it's a lot of fun until you get the bill.
Christopher Parker

———◇———

FEELING NATURE

Chapter Four

Our Unconscious Mind

The unconscious mind holds information you might not be aware of - from time to time, unconscious information may break through to your consciousness.

☼ Story 1

A young woman came to me feeling she was ugly. She said her mother called her a beanpole and siblings said she had a big nose. Even though this young woman was beautiful when she came to me, she still felt she was ugly.

This illustrates we carry our dark past with us all of our life, even when things change, until we change those old dark thoughts. I asked my client to say out loud, I am beautiful, three times right before she went to sleep each night for a week and then come back the following week to see me. She did. What she discovered during that week was that she was beautiful and not ugly at all. She became aware of her present, rather than her past. Her thoughts changed and she became aware of who she was in present times, rather than images she had created by her past.

A colleague once shared with me, "Feelings are part of our heritage, our past. While we are not free to choose the emotions that arose in us, we are free to choose when, where and how to express them, providing we know what they are."

I read this sentence in a book recently; it's impossible to feel bad while you are having happy thoughts.

Every time you catch yourself thinking negative thoughts or feeling bad listen to the warning signs that happened right before you began feeling bad or thinking negative thoughts. Think back to the very moment you changed your happy thoughts to unhappy ones. Something might have happened or someone might have said something that took you back to your past or childhood; a red flag is what I call it.

For example, one day I was walking home from a class feeling happy because I had just received a good grade, when I passed by a family sitting out in their front yard having a barbeque. There were three boys and a girl. The girl was sitting over by herself listening to her siblings while everyone else was joking and laughing. It hit me instantly. I started feeling sad and before I knew it my thoughts had changed. What that scene had taught me is that it took me back when I felt like the black sheep or outsider. When I recognized this, my thoughts went back to feeling good because I had long gotten over feeling like the outsider in my family. I knew I thought differently than them, but what I also knew was that they still loved me. So you see, sometimes old feelings rise that are of no longer use to us, but nonetheless still affect us. That is until we become aware of it and correct the thinking process; realizing it is still trying to cause us bad feelings when we know better.

———◇———

Quotes

Somewhere, right at the bottom of one's own being, one generally does know where one should go and what one should do.
Marie Louise vonFranz, colleague of Carl Jung

These are the colors which I tell you to paint with: faith, knowledge, reverence, kindness, fellowship, mildness, purity, goodness, brotherly love, sincerity, tranquility, fearlessness, cheerfulness, dignity and the whole band of colors which portray your soul, and which cure your bruises and heal your wounds and arrange your tangled hair and wash your face and instruct your eyes and cleanse your heart. The Acts of John

Awareness heals. Stephen Levine

Healing processes are built into all that lives, from plant to animal to man and woman. Matthew Fox

The worse things appear to be, the more we must fervently embrace the hope of the light which will follow. Sir George Trevelyan

The dark night of the soul comes just before revelation. When everything is lost, and all seems darkness, then comes the new life and all that is needed. Joseph Campbell

Understand that your life, as it is, contains the means to unconditionally cheer you up and cure you of depression and doubt. Chogyam Trungpa

Any time you react negatively to a person or to anything you must understand that this is your own unfinished business. Do you hear that?
Elisabeth Kubler-Ross

When we are mindful, touching deeply the present moment, we can see and listen deeply, and the fruits are always understanding, acceptance, love, and the desire to relieve suffering and bring joy.
Thich Nhat Hanh

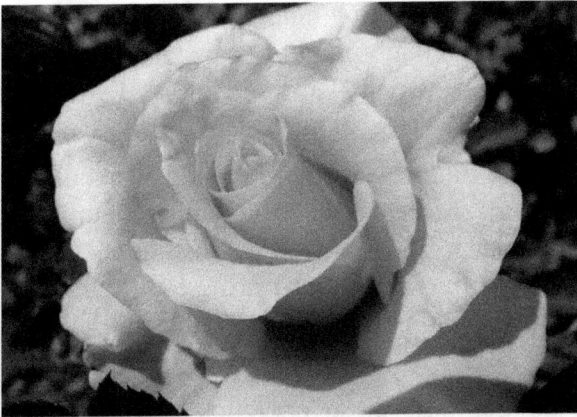

Nature gives back

Chapter Five

Our Health and Information

Freud once wrote *anger turned inward is depression.*

Fritz Pearl talked about anxiety and according to him it is the difference between the 'here and now' and 'in the future'. He claims the more we live in the future the more anxiety we are going to have. However, there are many different types of anxiety. Short term anxieties happen to most of us.

An example; let's say a dog bites us and then comes toward us again, short term anxiety might occur. Or if someone close to us is in an accident and we don't know if they're going to make it. These short term anxieties are the 'here and now'.

Anxiety 'in the future' is a disorder and it's about looking into the future and fearing what will happen. Sometimes it's a physical unbalance and we need medication to set our balance right, but sometimes it's about fearing the future and could be things that happened in our childhood that caused us emotional fears.

In order to get past these anxieties, we have to work on changing our thoughts and fears, or in some cases taking medication.

Anxiety never kills anyone so if we have anxiety about driving a car or flying on an airplane; we drive a car until we're comfortable or get on an airplane until we feel calm with it.

Yes, at first it might be powerfully uncomfortable and you might even have anxiety during these trials, but if you continue to do them, you will feel less anxiety after several attempts; that is if it isn't a physical unbalance.

Depression as we spoke about earlier might come from turned in anger or it might come from a physical unbalance. Some doctors say it comes from an emotional past or ways in which we handled certain emotional happenings in our life.

It could be projection as well, 'I think I'm ugly or I don't like myself.' In this case we need to change our thinking.

Things that we think can generate guilt and it creates an impulse to punish *self*. Hurt creates disruption and willingness to fight. A depressed person has a long list of what I should do.

Did you know how powerful your mind is? It is! It is powerful and it controls your body. Without our mind, our hand wouldn't know how to reach for an apple or Pepsi. If we think we can't do it, then we can't. If we think we aren't smart, then we aren't smart. Our thoughts control our mind's action. Our actions control our body.

☼ Story one

I was told by a client that she had an employee that told her when her spirit was happy she could work and not get tired because she was totally into her task, but if her spirit wasn't happy, by the time she got off work, she was so exhausted it took all her energy to get home.

Circle of Love

Everything is to be brought within the circle of Love
Annie Besant

—◇—

Full Spring has come to the mountain once again. All the trees are wrapped in their new green robes, and all the animals and birds are busy with new adventures and new families; new food and new fun. How alive this wonderful earth feels, born in the miracle of yet another spring.

There is a tiny little cove on the southern side of the mountain, and I'm eager to get there to see how everything is flourishing. Something catches my eye and I glance down to see a beautifully rounded blue shell - a robin's egg! I gently pick it up and notice jagged little places on it where the chick, eager for new life, pecked her way out of her confining circle to come forth to sunshine and warm breezes and new friends.

She comes forth from the egg to find herself encased within the larger circle of her new earth home, where she will find – as she did in her little egg – that all her needs will be provided for her, and that the *one life* which watches over and within her will protect and flourish that little spark within her which sings forth so sweetly and purely throughout the whole forest. She instinctively knew how to free herself from her small circle, in order to experience *life* more abundantly in tree and leaf, in sun and wind and rain shower.

We humans, too, are circles within circles; blood circling through our bodies, families circling around the hearth, societies and groups circling transcendent above their differences, pecking away at the now-constraining egg to come forth into ever-larger circles of love and mutual understanding.

As sure as the little chick pecks her way into a world that's just waiting for her with blessings and surprises everywhere, so we too instinctively 'peck' our way into a more abundant life of joy and blessings.

If we find that our thoughts are habitually negative; if our feelings are painful and constraining, then be sure that it's time for us to peck our way out of this tiny little circle which we instinctively know is too small for us. We weren't designed to stay within constricting little shells, wrapped up in negative thoughts and feelings. We were meant for much greater things - peace and joy and fulfillment, and, above all, love. And deep inside we know this.

It may be hard work. We may have to 'peck' for quite some time before we see the light break through the shell, but there is no need for discouragement, no need for a sense of frustration or failure. Just as the tiny robin makes her way into a larger, better world, so can we - so will we - because our natural human instincts will not let us ultimately rest in that tiny circle of negativity or despair. So why not start pecking today, now, this very moment? Leave the shell of those negative thoughts behind and before you know it, you'll be soaring on wings of happiness, just like our little cousin, the robin.

The new-born robin sings us a song of encouragement and cheer. She tells us that the same loving Life force that guided her out of her shell is also here to lend us a helping hand, so that we, too, can leave little old shells behind and soar on wings of hope and joy to a better life.

Quotes

The central secret is to know that the various human passions and feelings and emotions in the human heart are not wrong in themselves; only they have to be carefully controlled and given a higher and higher direction, until they attain the very highest condition of excellence.
Vivekananda, Indian spiritual teacher

Your answers lie inside you. All you need to do is look, listen, and trust. You'll tend to forget all this. You can remember anytime you wish.
 Anonymous

Dynamic psychology teaches that we can achieve inner health only through forgiveness – the forgiveness not only of others but also of ourselves.
Joshua Loth Liebman

Review the situations of your life and notice that for every negative encounter, there is a positive possibility. The ability to turn a negative into a positive is the essence of the process of living and learning.
Rabbi Shoni Labowitz

All of us dwell on the brink of the infinite ocean of life's creative power. We carry it within us: supreme strength, the fullness of wisdom, unquenchable joy. It is never thwarted and cannot be destroyed.
Huston Smith

Failure is not an end but a beginning, because it reveals something that will assist us in moving forward.
Wayne Teasdale

You always carry within yourself the very thing that you need for the fulfillment of your life purpose.
Malidoma Some

While the self may have experienced much pain and trauma during and after childhood, it is able to transmute that trauma into various expressions of insight, compassion, and innovation.
Robert Jay Lifton

Your world is perfect from the point of view of continually providing you with precisely the life experiences that you need for your overall development as a conscious being.
Ken Keyes

When problems arise, answers also arise.
Manly P. Hall

No matter what you're going through, the Ancestral Mind, grounded in the experiences of millions of years of evolution, can provide the emotional wisdom you need to endure and prevail.
Gregg D. Jacobs

First keep the peace within yourself, then you can also bring peace to others.
Thomas a'Kempis

The psyche has a remarkable ability to weather the storms of life and to renew itself.
John Welch, O. Carm.

Here is a key idea: stop thinking of your dark nights as problems and begin to see them as opportunities for change.
Thomas Moore

Inner guidance is always there inside us, and it is always correct, wise and loving. We may lose touch with it, or misinterpret it at times. We may try to push too hard and get ahead of ourselves. But our inner teacher never abandons us. We are never alone.
Shakti Gawain

Whatever your age, your upbringing, or your education, what you are made of is mostly unused potential.
George Leonard and Michael Murphy

We are all worth healing.
Joan Borysenko, PhD

This is not the first time anybody has ever been down the path you are walking. You create your reality out of an immense pool of energy, the energy of humankind. That wonderful connectedness of combined wisdom called humanity is a reservoir of awareness you can draw on.
Mary-Margaret Moore

Before all else, know that we are always in deep and energetic transformation. Always.
Z Budapest

Beyond your physical self, beyond your thoughts and emotions, there lies a realm within you that is pure potential....This part of you is interwoven with everything else that exists, and with everything yet to come.
Deepak Chopra

Every painful event contains in itself a seed of growth and liberation.
Anthony deMello

We need deliberately to call to mind the joys of our journey. Perhaps we should try to write down the blessings of one day. We might begin: we could never end: there are not pens or paper enough in all the world.
George A. Buttrick

Now the real treasure, to end our misery and trials, is never far away; it lies buried in the innermost recess of our own home, in the life and warmth-giving center of the structure of our existence, our heart of hearts - if we can only dig.
Heinrich Zimmer

If one is sincere when confronted with difficulties, the heart can penetrate the meaning of the situation. And once we have gained inner mastery of a problem, it will come about naturally that the action we take will succeed.
I Ching

In moments of darkness and pain remember all is cyclical. Sit quietly behind your wooden door: Spring will come again.
Loy Ching Yuen

In fact, the desire for joy is inherently stronger than the fear of sadness.
Thomas Aquinas

Use the light that is in you to revert to your natural clearness of sight.
The Tao Te King

Stop thinking of yourself as plunged in misery. Have you forgotten how fortunate you have been in many ways?
Boethius

Do not think meanly of yourself and do not despair of perfection.
Moses Maimonides

We ought therefore in every work and application of things eagerly to aspire, imagine, hope and most firmly believe, for that will be a very great help.
Paracelsus

There is an inner direction and meaning that inheres at the transpersonal level in every life.
Shirley J. Nicholson

Indeed, no one ever sincerely cries for light in vain.
Geoffrey Hodson

The way through the present crisis is to learn to understand ourselves.
Laurence and Phoebe Bendit

With me it was as when a seed is hidden in the earth. Contrary to all reason, it grows up in storm and rough weather. In the winter, all is dead, and reason says, 'Everything is ended for it'. But the precious seed within me sprouted and grew green, oblivious of all storms.
Jacob Boehme

Joy is ours as something which eternally abides through all the changes of circumstance, of light and shadow, because it is of the very essence of life.
Hugh I'anson Fausset

We cannot win enlightenment for ourselves unless we are seeking it for all. Equally, however, we cannot be loving and kind to others, unless we are the same to ourselves.
Hugh I'anson Fausset

The older and deeper all-pervading joy is there...even when evil or pain is being endured on the level of consciousness controlled by individualized existence. Joy is always in the revels of the atoms and molecules making up the flesh and blood of the sufferer, in the swing of the planet on which he or she stands, in the sun which gives warmth and life. It is there...and can be tapped even in the darkest suffering.
Robert Ellwood

My true nature and its power will rise to my assistance. If I trust my true nature all the way, my heart will vibrate to its music of truth.
Cyril H. Boynes

Every experience is valuable; nothing is wasted, even if it appears so, for silently the seed is developing.
Geoffrey Hodson

Beneficent forces ever and anon have enabled humanity to find a refuge from every peril and to outlive the longest night.
Carl Jung

There is only one certainty – nothing can put out the light within.
Carl Jung

The psyche is a self-regulating system that maintains itself in equilibrium as the body does. Every process that goes too far immediately and inevitably calls forth a compensatory activity.
Carl Jung

When the confusion is at its height a new revelation comes.
Carl Jung

Our instincts have ridden so infinitely many times, unharmed, over the problems that arise [in] life that we may be sure the transformation processes which make the transition possible have long been prepared in the unconscious and are only waiting to be released.
Carl Jung

If we can really accept ourselves, we can feed and develop ourselves; to expect anything else is like expecting a cast-off child to thrive.
Carl Jung

Wisdom is the comforter of all psychic suffering.
Carl Jung

Intuition is one of the basic functions of the psyche, namely perception of the possibilities inherent in a situation.
Carl Jung

Flowers are friends

Wish upon a star

Chapter Six

Quotes and Poems to Think About

A happy person is not a person in a certain set of circumstances, but rather a person with a certain set of attitudes.

Scottish Proverb

We do not choose our circumstances or trials, but we do choose how we respond to them. It is through struggle that we find redemption and self-knowledge.

Condoleezza Rice

Human beings, by changing the inner attitudes of their minds, can change the outer aspects of their lives. William James, American Psychologist

Nothing can bring you peace but yourself.

Ralph Waldo Emerson

Just as the physical sun lightens and warms the universe, so, in the human body, there is in the heart a sun like Arcanum from which life and warmth stream forth.

Carl Jung

One thing that comes out in myths is that at the bottom of the abyss comes the voice of salvation. At the darkest moment comes the light. Joseph Campbell

Intuition is one of the basic functions of the psyche, namely perception of the possibilities inherent in a situation. Carl Jung

We are not prisoners. No traps or snares are set about us, and there is nothing which should intimidate or worry us. We are set down in life as in the element to which we best correspond. All the dragons of our lives are princesses who are only waiting to see us once beautiful and brave. Perhaps everything terrible is in its deepest being something helpless that wants help from us. Rainer Marie Rilke, poet

The process of becoming conscious always implies becoming aware of one's real personality and of its pre-destined wholeness. It is as if there were a central image working behind all manifestations of life and determining them. The wholeness is achieved in proportion as the central image determines every single act of the personality, and finds therein its full and undisturbed actualization. Gerhard Adler

———◇———

All heaven's glory is within
And so is hell's fierce burning,
You must yourself decide
In which direction
You are turning.

Angelus Silesius, 'The book of Angelus Silesius'

The greater part of our happiness or misery depends on our dispositions, and not on our circumstances. We carry the seeds of the one or the other about with us in our minds wherever we go.

Martha Washington, 'Letters'

Angelus Silesius was a German mystic of the 17th century. Martha Washington was the wife of the first president of the United States. They lived in two totally different worlds, and surely they saw the world differently in many ways, but here was something they could both agree with. To a great extent, we do indeed create the reality which we experience. Our habitual attitudes shape and define our circumstances and the way we perceive them. Almost every scripture, every saint and philosopher agreed about this inner truth, and this book will introduce to you many of our friends from the past who have good advice on how to handle and direct our emotions.

We do indeed have the ability - and the responsibility - to see that our attitudes and dispositions toward Life are sound, whole, reasonable, and oriented toward emotional health and well-being. And it's really not as difficult to do this as we may think.

In the final analysis, we do reap what we sow. In any given moment of Life, each one of us is poised at the crossroads, given the power to choose either the heaven of truth within our beings, or the hell of negativity. In every life, no matter how dark the circumstances, we can always find some things to be grateful for, and at the same time we can find things to complain about, become angry or fearful about. It all depends where we choose to put our focus.

At this point, you may be thinking to yourself, "Ahh, but you have no idea how really dark my circumstances are." True, there are some situations which may seem utterly hopeless. Yet even in the deepest pit of despair, the heaven within you can still be found. Let's listen to what another of our friends from the past has to say:

Truly I have looked into the very heart of darkness and refused to yield to its paralyzing influence. What if all dark, discouraging moods come across my way as thick as the dry leaves of autumn? I know the desert leads to God as surely as the fruitful orchards. I use my will, choose life and reject its opposite, nothingness.

Helen Keller,

Helen spent most of her life unable to see, hear or speak. Surely few lives have been touched with darkness like hers was. And yet Helen was still able to see and consistently focus on the positive things in her life. She chose to think positive, even in such a seemingly hellish position. May her example awaken in us the desire to see this world in all its marvelous possibilities, instead of giving way to chronic anger, fear, or despair.

Our state of consciousness is determined by our habitual attitude, and this attitude can always be modified, changed, transmuted into something better than it had been before. Old habits do die hard, but as we practice seeing the good and true in life, we will begin to see that we really do have the power to control, direct, and shape our thoughts and feelings.

Angelus, Martha and Helen are here with us in Spirit to encourage us on to give birth to our new selves, and there are many other old friends who can help us to become the calm, centered, truly happy people we all want to be. Let us follow in their footsteps and open the door to a brand new day for each of us, following the truth which indeed will set us free from damaging thoughts and emotions.

Listen within

Creation's Choice

In the beginning is every moment
Every second is birth anew
Creation is a Living Song -
And this moment is up to you.
Every heartbeat is Spirit's rhythm
Dancing sure on the present wave
We choose the beat we like and either
Wound or kill or save.
Ever on the beginning is always
And the future unfolds sublime
When we choose to birth Creation's plan
With a calm and peaceful Mind.

JoAnn Kite
© 2003

The whole future, the whole history of the world, ultimately springs from hidden sources in individuals. We make our own epoch.

Carl Jung - Civilization in Transition

———◇———

We must regain our respect for our uniqueness of mind and power of will so that we may utilize them to aid us in examining and selecting the most sound and growth-producing alternatives among the many choices the future will offer. Leo F. Buscaglia

You have to *choose* to make the best of a difficult situation and to trust that a reason beyond your understanding is always at work. Caroline Myss

What we need to do is make conscious choices and take attitudes. Caroline Myss

We are not the victims or the effects of uncontrollable external circumstances: the journey of transformation is within us. Therefore, we choose the destination. Ralph Metzner

We choose. We choose what carries energy in our lives. We choose what we pay attention to. We choose what mental and emotional impulses and responses drive us. Christina Baldwin

We always have a choice. We can let the garden of our life grow wild and unattended until it fills with weeds, or we can take up the proper tools and tend to our garden until we create a place of unimaginable loveliness. John Marks Templeton

You can choose to think positive thoughts or negative thoughts. You can choose to feel happy or sad. You can choose to see the positive in a negative situation, or the negative in a positive situation. Rabbi Shoni Labowitz

And who do I now choose to be? This is the only question that matters, and this is what your soul is using your life to decide, every moment. Neale Donald Walsch

There are only two ways to live your life. One is as though nothing is a miracle. The other is as though everything is a miracle. Albert Einstein

In the end, love and fear are the only feelings there are. Life brings you a constant stream of opportunities to choose between the two. Neale Donald Walsch

The final forming of a person's character lies in their own hands. Anne Frank

We are continually engaged in the evolution of self and world – and we have the power to choose, moment by moment, between that which gives life and that which deals death. Parker J. Palmer

One need remain in hell no longer than one chooses to; we can rise to any heaven we ourselves choose; and when we choose so to rise, all the higher powers of the Universe combine to help us heavenward. R. W. Trine

We get in life that which we focus on. Continual focus on darkness leads us, as individuals and as a society, further into darkness. Focus on the light brings us into the light." Marianne Williamson

Anger at wrongs must be transformed into shared pain at common suffering, and into resolve toward change…Conflict must be transformed into creative, cooperative peace. Leonard J. Bowen,

It is better to light a single candle than to curse the darkness. Motto of the Christophers, quoted by John Marks Templeton

There is no such thing as a problem without a gift for you in its hands. John Marks Templeton

Difficulties strengthen you if you will allow them to do so. They will permit you to love and be loved abundantly.
Patricia Devlin

You are never alone. There is always a sacred being available within you who will help you overcome obstacles with wisdom, understanding, compassion, and strength.
Rabbi Shoni Labowitz

Review the situations of your life and notice that for every negative encounter, there is a positive possibility. The ability to turn a negative into a positive is the essence of the process of living and learning.
Rabbi Shoni Labowitz

Each moment of your life is a holy moment, a moment of creation. Each moment is a new beginning. In each, you are born again.
Neale Donald Walsch

All of us dwell on the brink of the infinite ocean of life's creative power. We carry it within us: supreme strength, the fullness of wisdom, unquenchable joy. It is never thwarted and cannot be destroyed.
Huston Smith,

Your trials did not come to punish you, but to awaken you.
Paramahansa Yogananda

We are one

Chapter Seven

Why do we stay in Abusive Relationships?

A client of mine came to see me confused and depressed because she said her husband abused her. She continued to tell me when she was young and feisty she used to say, *if a man ever abused me, I would immediately leave him, but now I know those words mean nothing until you have experienced it.*

She shared with me that they were married seven years before he first hit her; after that it never stopped. Many times she would end up in the hospital with a broken nose or arm. She said, "I had stopped working when we married and even though I wanted to leave, I did not feel I could support myself, so I stayed."

Many women have told me that their abusive husbands had refused to let them have friends or to work so by the time they felt they had had enough, their self-esteem was so low that they were afraid to leave.

This happens to men as well. Men have come to me with the same stories.

Abuse, whether it happens to men or women, is something that happens and when it does, we who have not had that experience think it is easy and so we say, *just leave!*

I believe our thoughts make us stay in situations that are not healthy for us. In many cases, it is our belief systems that cause us to remain in situations. Sometimes it is the programming we got while growing up. Sometimes because of being told we were not worthy, we begin to believe it and our thoughts of fear began to grow. Our thoughts of past statements; *you are stupid*! *You cannot do anything right! You are so ugly!* We hear them in our head; we feel them in our hearts. Until we feel confused, frustrated and have no self-esteem what so ever. Because of these feelings and thoughts, we tend to either blame others or think we are failures.

What do we do? We change our thoughts. We repeat over and over every day that we can support ourselves, we do not have to take the abuse anymore, until one day our thoughts are changed and we take action. In some cases, we have to ask for help. There are shelters; there are people who are willing to help. In some cases we walk and talk to ourselves changing our past experiences by visualizing them different in our mind.

Chapter Eight

Change Your State of Mind

The main thing you need to do is trust the Universe, trust yourself and remember to always have faith.

When you let go of your limiting thoughts, it opens doors for you, it sends you off into the melody of your life. It not only allows you to be in better physical health, it allows you to be in better mental health. With both of these, it attracts positive things to enter your life where you can smile and feel the music of all things and people around you.

If you are out of shape and want to get in shape, then begin to visualize it in your mind and within moments it will open to the door to reach that goal. Life truly is what you make it to be.

My father told me all of my life; *what you think is what you are.* He had a wisdom I didn't know when I was younger, but as I got older, I began to see what wisdom he had in those words.

I also have a son who once told me when I told him I couldn't do it. He smiled his great smile and said, "Mom, just visualize it and then you can." Little did I know the words I had taught him would come back to teach me.

If you want something, believe it is on its way to you, and you will be amazed at how this simple thing works.

I had a friend who was going through a divorce and was

suffering. My heart went out for her when I saw the pain on her face each time I saw her. One night I rested in bed thinking how I could get the message of believing and positive thought to her in order to change her suffering. After meditation I knew what I would tell her. So that afternoon, I said, "Do you want to try something with me?"

She smiled and said, "Sure."

I said, "Let's go shopping today and believe and think that everywhere we go, we'll get front row parking."

She looked at me as through to say, *are you crazy? We can't get front row parking everywhere we go.* Guess what? Everywhere we went and let me tell you, we went to a lot of stores, we got front row parking at every store. It was just a little illustration of positive thinking; having faith in visualization, but it worked and from that day on, my friend started using it and trying it on different other things in her life. Before long, she was out telling others about it and others to telling others and so it went.

One night I was lying in bed thinking about how wonderful it would be if the whole world would visualize peace and happiness. Wouldn't it be great? I think it would and you know what, if we tell others about this wonderful thing, just in our own little world and each one of them told those in their own little world, it would soon get across all of the world ~ *Positive Thinking.*

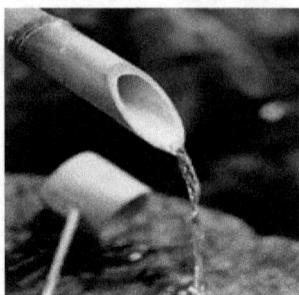

Chapter Nine

The Power of the Mind

I read an article recently that talked about why some minds stay sharp despite aging, it also talked about a study of the brains of people who stayed mentally sharp into their 80s.

The brains of some elderly people with super-sharp memory seem to escape the formation of destructive "tangles" that increase with normal aging and peak in people with Alzheimer's.
Source: Galaxy

The article went on to say in a presentation at the National Meeting of the American Chemical Society, Changiz Geula, principal investigator of the Northwestern University Super Aging Project and a professor of neuroscience at the Cognitive Neurology and Alzheimer's Disease Center - explained their discovery of elderly people with sharp memories. The so-called "super-aged" individuals who somehow escaped brain dysfunctions'. The *tangles* as they call them, or dysfunctions', consist of an abnormal form of a protein called *tau* that damages and eventually kills nerve cells, which has advancing age and peak in people with Alzheimer's disease.

There is now evidence that some individuals are immune to *tangle formation* or dysfunctions'. It said, evidence also supports the notion that the presences of *tangles* may influence cognitive performance.

Geula said that this new study is unique in its spotlight on what's right with the brains of older people. It seeks insights into what lifestyle, genetics, or other factors may protect super-aged individuals from the age-related memory loss that affects most other people. Interesting enough, what scientists found that super-aged people seem to fall into two sub-groups:

1. Those who are almost immune to *tangle formation* and those that have *few tangles*. And by the way, this group of super-aged; their brains are virtually clean, which doesn't happen in normal aged people.
2. The second group seems to get *tangles,* but it's less than the amount in the normal elderly. Otherwise, they seem to be protected against its effects.

Geula said, we might ask why one subgroup is immune to tangle formation and the other seems to be immune to its effects. The thought is that it may be environment, lifestyle, and genetics may be key factors. An example he gave was that some super-aged individuals might have a genetic predisposition to being super-aged, while others may help preserve high brain function by maintaining a healthy diet or staying physically active. On the other hand, others may keep mental decline on hold by keeping the brain itself active: By reading books, writing, playing crossword puzzles, or engaging in other mentally demanding activities.

My thought is that if we read more, write more, or simply engage in mental activities, couldn't it also be what we think about as well? If our thoughts are positive thoughts, we already know we have fewer heart attacks, less stress and our bodies are healthier. This is certainly something to think about seriously.

Let's talk about another article I read on the power of the mind and the subconscious mind power which are described in many different ways. The article said in the psychosomatic sense mind power is labeled as ability to have emotions, imagination, memory, and will. Whereas in the subconscious mind power, it is tagged as part of the normal individual's personality in which mental grips function without consciousness under normal waking conditions.

Okay, let's stay with this until we reach the conclusion of this matter; Stay with me.

Mind power is our *conscious mind*, the way we think. With the mind and its thoughts; it cannot uniformly think negative and positive thoughts at the same time. One will rule the other.

Let us go farther into this matter; since our mind reflects habitual thoughts it is important and our own necessary responsibility to control our mind and brain with positive emotions; thoughts and energy as the ruling factors in our mind. When we think, *it is important to believe in what we are thinking*. Now how can we do that if we think from our conditional mind? You know the one that conditioned us as we were wee babies from adulthood. Okay. Believing in the right now what you think that will manifest your reality. However, if we go back to our dark past and statements made to us and react with them, we are not in the present reality of our thoughts. Our thoughts and beliefs will create the outcome of *our* now. Do you see it now? It is *most important* to stay aware to the reflections you are thinking

But let's go even farther, if you look at our conscious and or subconscious we see it as a dual system that includes our power of thought; *the brain*. Trust me when I say we all have subconscious mind power. We are more in control of our mind and body than we've been lead to believe. We are in charge of ourselves; that is if we take the driver's wheel and use it.

Believe this – what you think and believe is what your subconscious mind power will produce. Every thought feeds habitually by your mind will activate your subconscious mind to generate those thoughts and energy whether good or bad into your life. Think about it; this is how you're present and what happens in your future is created. Now, let's go to your past ~ does it control thoughts in your present day time? Yes it does; that is unless you've re-visualized those past thoughts into new fresh changed ones, and even then they will always be with you, but you've chosen to make the changed one more present with change.

An old movie comes to mind where Steve Martin and Goldie Hawn pair up for the first time in director Frank Oz's romantic comedy of an architect and waitress who spin *wild tales* about being married to each other. However, it comes to light that their stories aren't entirely false. When Davis (Martin) tries to throw out unwanted house sitter Gwen (Hawn) from his lovely but unoccupied house, he soon realizes that Gwen's romantic lies to the locals about their whirlwind courtship and wedding have captured the townsfolk's hearts and made jealous the woman who turned down Davis's marriage proposal months before. Seeing the chance to win back his sweetheart, Becky, Davis agrees to let Gwen stay in the house while they pretend to be married. As Gwen's bright stories bring Becky and a deserved promotion, Davis must figure out how much of his pretend marriage truly is a sham.

This movie illustrates that Goldie Hawn visualizes and pretends to be Steve Martin's wife and as it turns out, she in reality becomes his wife in the movie.

Sometimes your Greatest Misery is your Greatest Happiness

Chapter Ten

More Poems and quotes

Happy Things

When you reach high,
talk about happy things.
Lift the world,
give it happy things
Speak of magical happy thoughts,
which will bring you happy things.
Pattimari
© 2010

Positive Thoughts

There he was
a smile
a bright day
he slept well
because he had positive thoughts
pattimari
© 2010

Still be Glad

Through toil and trails
be glad
still
remember the grass grows
water flows
flowers blossom
warm winds blow
and you are alive!
pattimari

Share the sunbeams

Share the warmth
talk about the dawning day
smile at the thorns
for you have chosen the best
to live with happy thoughts
pattimari
© 2010

Your Power
In the month of May
remember sorrow
can turn to gladness
comfort others
and tell him
thoughts can be changed
because love abounds
Pattimari

Sing a Happy Song

When the days are overcast,
sing a happy song
Smile at the heavens,
give to those in need
Lift up your arms,
and sing a happy song.
Pattimari
©2010

Make a Difference

Slap your hands together
so things get better
Open your heart wide
to those closed up tight
Smile
when someone frowns at you
hold your happy thoughts
deep inside of you
When the dark past
surrounds you with fear
change them to courage and hope
and happy thoughts
all around you.

Pattimari
© 2010

Ring in Positive Things

When you see sadness,
ring out with your love
When darkness comes your way,
turn on the light
Ring in the nobler things
with warmness and purer laws
When the mind is sapped,
Ring in positive things
Ring out darkness and false pride
dark memories of childhood things
Ring in love and truth
Ring out lust of money

and all those things
Ring in positive things.
pattimari
copyright, 2010

☐

Picture What You Want It To Be

When your days are blue,
picture it in a better way.
When things go wrong,
move over to the right
When tears fall
let your laughter
ring out!
pattimari
© 2010

I would rather be ashes than dust!

I would rather that my spark should burn out in a brilliant
blaze than it should be stifled by dry rot. I would rather be a
superb meteor, every atom of me in magnificent glow, than a
sleepy and permanent person. The proper function of man is to
live, not to exist. I shall not waste my days in trying to prolong
them. I shall use my positive mind and be in the time.
unknown

Chapter Eleven

Stories of Value

Making Sandcastles

Hot sun. Salty air. Rhythmic waves.

A little boy is on his knees scooping and packing the sand with plastic shovels into a bright blue bucket. Then he upends the bucket on the surface and lifts it. And, to the delight of the little architect, a castle tower is created.

All afternoon he will work; spooning out the moat, packing the walls, bottle tops will be sentries and popsicles sticks will be bridges. A sandcastle will be built.

Big city. Busy streets. Rumbling traffic.

A man is in his office. At his desk he shuffles papers into stacks and delegates assignments. He cradles the phone on his shoulder and punches the keyboard with his fingers. Numbers are juggled and contracts are signed and much to the delight of the man, a profit is made.

All his life he will work. Formulating the plans. Forecasting the future. Annuities will be sentries. Capital gains will be bridges. An empire will be built.

Two builders of two castles. They have much in common. They shape granules into grandeurs. They see nothing and make something. They are diligent and determined. And for both - the tide will rise and the end will come.

Yet that is where the similarities cease - For the boy sees the end while the man ignores it. Watch the boy as the dusk approaches.

As the waves near, the wise child jumps to his feet and begins to clap. There is no sorrow. No fear. No regret. He knew this would happen. He is not surprised. And when the great breaker crashes into his castle and his masterpiece is sucked into the sea, he smiles. He smiles, picks up his tools, takes his father's hand, and goes home.

The grownup, however, is not so wise. As the wave of year's collapses on his castle he is terrified. He hovers over the sandy monument to protect it. He blocks the waves from the walls he has made. Salt-water soaked and shivering he snarls at the incoming tide.

"It's my castle," he defies.

The ocean need not respond. Both know to whom the sand belongs...
I don't know much about sandcastles. But children do. Watch them and learn. Go ahead and build, but build with a child's heart. When the sun sets, and the tides take - applaud. Salute the process of life and go home.

Author, unknown

Our Inner Treasure

Our instincts have ridden so infinitely many times, unharmed, over the problems that arise in life that we may be sure the transformation processes have long been prepared in the unconscious and are only waiting to be released. In the human being, the darkness calls forth the helpful light.
Carl Jung

There is a precious and living *Treasure* beating deep in your human heart and mind, a *Treasure* more sparkling and precious than all the world's jewels. And you may tap into this vibrant *Treasure* within you any time you choose. Any time you need strength to face a difficulty, or wisdom to know how to meet a situation, this inner *Treasure*, this *living energy*, will come to meet you with healing in its wings.

Some call this treasure the higher self. Some call it intuition, or inner Tao. Some call it the Collective Unconscious, our one ancestral mind which has been with us and growing us for millennia. As Carl Jung says, "If it were permissible to personify the unconscious, we might call it a collective human being combining the characteristics of both sexes, transcending youth and age, birth and death, and, from having at its command a human experience of one or two million years, almost immortal."

Life and our parents gifted us not only with the DNA to grow marvelously coordinated bodies, composed of trillions of cells which work in harmony and near perfect coordination, but they have also gifted us with the combined wisdom of all of our ancestors. Each and every one of us shares in this ancient, almost immortal ancestral heritage of wisdom, and it is there for us whenever we need it. And even when we don't even understand it or ask for its help, it will meet us in our darkest hours and carry us safely and securely to joy and peace and fresh new beginnings.

As Jung explains, "Instinctive defense mechanisms have been developed which automatically intervene when the danger is greatest. These mechanisms come into play whenever the need is great." And Gerhard Adler, another prominent psychologist of the last century, realized that "The unconscious contains all the factors which are necessary for the integration of the personality. It possesses, as it were, a superior knowledge of our real needs in regard to their integration and the ways to achieve them."

So, how do we begin to dig into our inner selves in order to find this buried, precious Treasure? Our emotions have ridden over us, perhaps, so many times that we can no longer see any way out. We may have fallen so far into a chronic negativity that we haven't the strength left to do some sort of thorough self-analysis. We may be sunk in depression, in total darkness, and may have lost all hope of ever seeing the light once again. Still, there is hope. Still there is this *Living Treasure* working within us, and there is something in us which knows this, and will determine to find a better way to live, no matter what. But how do we tap it?

John Sanford was a 20th century Jungian psychologist who had great insight into our human nature, being an expert in our inner workings. His advice to all those who would leave their world of darkness and futility behind are as follows: "New paths must be cut and new habits formed. The drive of the psyche must be concentrated on new objectives; and the old paths; left to themselves must fade and die."

Here is the door which opens the inner room which contains the *Treasure*. We must begin by thinking the opposite of those negative old emotions. We must remember that every single emotion which humanity as a whole has ever experienced lies potentially within you and can be called upon to help you in your hour of need. We must concentrate on new objectives, new paths toward maturity and balance of feeling, and a masterly control of our thoughts and moods. As Charles Leadbeater, a 19th century natural psychologist wrote, "There is plenty of good in the world, and it is better to think of that, for your thought strengthens that of which you think."

The tide of our human evolution is on our side in this endeavor. We may feel like the old sage Francois Fenelon felt when he said, "But how can I help being constantly self-engrossed when a crowd of anxious thoughts disturb me and set me ill at ease?" But then he goes on to answer his own question, "If you are steadfast in resisting them (negative thoughts) whenever you become conscious of their existence, by degrees you will get free."

Almost two thousand years ago, Plotinus had the key to unlock the *Treasure* room: "Withdraw into yourself and look", he says, "and if you do not find yourself beautiful yet, act as does the creator of a statue that is to be made beautiful. He cuts away here, he smoothes there, he makes this line lighter, this other purer, until a lovely face has grown upon his work. So do you also; cut away all that is excessive, straighten all that is crooked, bring light to all that is overcast, labor to make all one glow of beauty and never cease chiseling your statue, until there shall shine out in you from it the splendor of virtue, until you see the perfect goodness surely established in the stainless shrine."

In this book, Pattimari and I share with you a sampling of the thoughts of our brothers and sisters from all time and places, people who have found this inner *Treasure* and have shared their jewels of human wisdom with us. Taken to heart, and read in a quiet and open manner, these wise voices of our common humanity can be a means toward the healing of our negative and unwanted thoughts and emotions. They can lead us to the inner *Treasure*, that power house of love and wisdom that wants to be found, and will be found, always, whenever the darkness calls for it.

"In all chaos there is a cosmos, in all disorder a secret order, in all caprice a fixed law."

Carl Jung, "Archetypes of the Collective Unconscious"

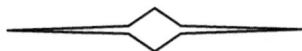

Chapter Twelve

How Meditation Makes your Mind Clearer

When we meditate we stimulated many hidden gifts that we never knew existed. We become closer to answering life's major questions.

Our mind is clear and our brains work better giving us enhanced levels of thinking. In fact, in scientific and medical testing the results showed people who meditate have superior brain power. Many of history's greatest inventors, philosophers, and scientists received their inventive, transforming ideas during their daily meditative sessions. It also showed that mediators produce more euphoric brain chemicals.

Meditation enhances your sleeping habits, leaving you refreshed and rejuvenated when you wake each morning. Some even say that a mediator needs less sleep, but there isn't any known test that proves this claim. However, I will say when I meditated 30 minutes a day I slept less and still felt refreshed.

It is a known fact that the anger, depression, anxiety and sadness levels were lower when one meditates.

A few years ago, we did a survey and had a group of people meditate for a month 15 minutes a day. At the end of the month, 90 percent of the people said they felt happier, more satisfied and content with their lives. One said her anxiety disorder left and she was overjoyed.

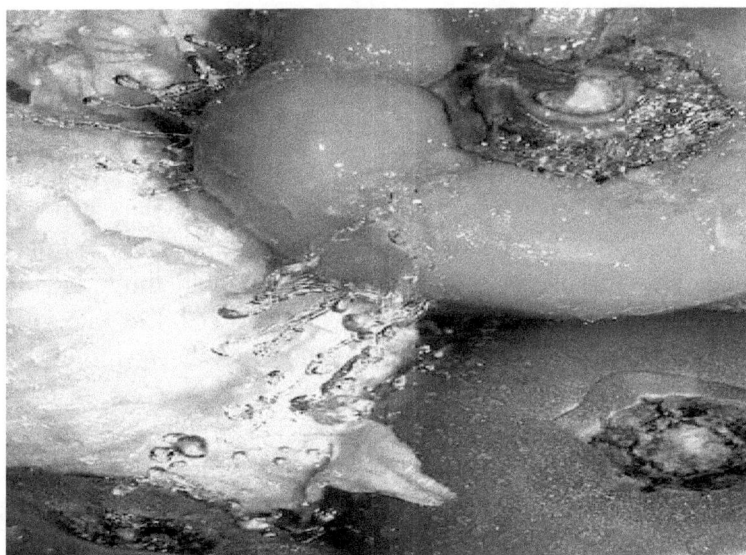

Eating good is important

Chapter Thirteen

Our Thoughts

Thoughts and their power have astonishing forces in which we can use to make our life a better one.

If you take a look at our world and the state it is in, we know it's because of human shared thinking. The result of our thoughts and where we allow our thoughts to go is where we will be in the reality of our life right now. We can be; happy or unhappy, positive or negative - have poverty or riches, peace or war. It is up to our thoughts and where we allow them to go. Whether it's thinking as a nation or individual thinking, our thoughts are the result of where we are in our life this very moment. Otherwise, what a person thinks is the results of all their actions.

"Do not under estimate the Power of Thoughts. Just as water has the power to shift and mold earths landscape, your thoughts have the power to shift and mold the landscape of your life."
Chuck Danes

You can discover the power of positive thought and begin to transform your entire life right now. How? - By changing your thoughts. What we think is what we are right now in our life.

Have you wondered where your thoughts come from or how much power they have? Or how it is shaping your life right now? It is. Our thoughts come from our past and how we learned to develop thoughts. We listened to our teachers, our parents, our siblings and our peers and create thoughts. Some were negative thoughts while some were positive ones, but both entered our life as thoughts when we listened to people talk in our life. I had a client who actually thought she was stupid. She had no self-esteem whatsoever. She thought she couldn't go to college or pass their exams, so she didn't even try. In a session long after seeing her for weeks, I asked her where she got the thought that she was stupid. She said, "Because I am." I said, "I know you think you are, but when did you begin thinking you were?" She hummed and hawed for a moment and then she said, "I guess when my father said I was stupid because I dropped a dish on his foot. Then once when my teacher told me I'd never amount to anything because I wasn't smart enough to be quiet." I thought for a moment and then I said, "So you still think you're stupid from past statements; statements that were made when you were a child?" She nodded and then widened her eyes in surprise. I asked her to take a little test for me. I reached into my briefcase and brought out a test I often gave to some clients and handed it to her. She dug in her purse and came out with a pen and began to take the test. When she finished, I was amazed at her perfect score. She was too. I proceeded to tell her that it was time to change her thoughts to "I'm smart." From that day on, I saw a change in her. She seemed happier and often smiled when I greeted her. Then one day she asked me if I thought there were other past thoughts she had been taught that affected her life today. I chuckled and said, "Absolutely! We all have those past thoughts that we have to change." Before she left that day, she turned and said to me, "I'm going to change all of those past dark thoughts!" I smiled and said, "Good."

Our thoughts direct our life and cause us to mold who we think we are. We can remold those old ones and make new positive ones. We can literally change our whole life. When you really look at that statement, there is no stopping you from becoming and living exactly the way you'd like to be or live.

When you consider every event, condition and circumstance in your life clarifies it is the result of your creative power – your thoughts. (*The way you thought in your past.*) The way you think, is the way you'll view yourself and others for that matter. Isn't it time to change those old thoughts to new fresh ones? - Ones that can make you a happier person? I say yes, if you want to have a happy life and a successful one.

When you understand you can implement the power of your thoughts and realize how vital it is to do so, you will
begin to find that dream you often dreamed, and you will find your thoughts changing to the positive. You will look at yourself differently. You will feel better about yourself.
If you want to think about something even bigger than you and I, let's think about human evolution. Wouldn't it be a much better world if we all changed our negative thinking? Would we judge others so easily? Would we criticize so easily? I doubt it.
If we could fully grasp and understand how the power of thoughts mold and shape your life, you may work toward changing them. My greatest hope is that this book JoAnn, Charlotte, and I are writing will do just that for you. This is the whole purpose of this book – to give you valuable information to make changes in your life so that you can be a happier person.

Remember the old saying~ an apple a day will keep the doctor away?

Chapter Fourteen

Helpful Hints for Treasure Hunting and Short Stories

In this chapter you will hear what some of your brothers and sisters from many times and places have to tell you about how to create and maintain an emotionally healthy and happy outlook on life. As you read, consider this: These wise words are not just in the book you have in your hands. They are also resonating deep within your own being, as part of the one collective human wisdom, that wonderful Treasure which is within each and every one of us. If we take their hands, in spirit, and listen with openness and deep reflection to the wisdom they bring, we may learn how to walk through our fears and negativities and come out the other side into the *real* world of peace and love, happiness and true joy.

One cannot love and fear at the same time anymore. Our consciousness has become too differentiated for such contradictions.
Carl Jung, 20th century psychologist

There are only two factors in life:
   1. The sense of Unity with others and with Nature - which covers Love, Faith, Courage, Truth and so forth.
   2. Non-perception of the same - which covers enmity, fear, hatred, self-pity, cruelty, jealousy, meanness, etc. Edward Carpenter, 19th century author

If error, not truth, is the diet of the mind, then the heart gorges itself on poison and is doomed to frustration and despair. Only truth is light for the eyes and goal for the heart. We are real, we live in a world of real things, and our hearts are not to be nourished on fantasies or nightmares but on Realities.
Thomas Aquinas, 13th century theologian

Believe that life is worth living, and your belief will help create the fact.
William James, early 20th century psychologist

Both fear and greed can become so developed as to virtually imprison a person in his outlook. The liberating forces are love and courage, forever the saviors of humanity.
Clara Codd, contemporary author

My brethren, let us not be double minded, but remain steadfast in hope. For the reason some do not find peace is because they give way to human fears.
Clement, 2nd century Christian author

It is cynicism and fear that freeze life; it is faith that thaws it out, releases it, sets it free.
Harry Emerson Fosdick, 20th century spiritual psychologist

The power of fear is enormously aggravated by the thought form we ourselves have built of our own individual fears and phobias. This thought form grows in power as we pay attention to it, for "energy follows thought.
Alice A Bailey, 20th century esotericist

All infractions of love and equity in our social relations are aggressively punished. They are punished by fear.
Ralph W Emerson, 19th century essayist

The steadfast, loving attention to some aspect of the Transcendent Reality perceived leads to growth toward new levels and transmutation of character. Carl Jung
We must always change, renew, rejuvenate ourselves; otherwise we harden.
Goethe, 19th century poet and philosopher

To live happily is an inward power of the soul. Marcus Aurelius, Roman emperor and philosopher
The Mind is master over every kind of fortune; itself acts in both ways, being the cause of its own happiness and misery.
Seneca, Roman author

Whatever one implants firmly in the mind becomes the essential thing.
The Kabbalah

Conscience is an interior perception of what is good and true, and acting contrary to it causes anxiety.
Emanuel Swedenborg, 18th century visionary and author

Deeds and thoughts of violence automatically draw weight and darkness into the soul; those of gentleness lighten, both its color and its weight.
Joseph Campbell, 20th century mythologist

Thoughts Have Remarkable Powers

Thought can heal diseases and change the mindset of people. It can work wonders. The speed of thought is incredible and dynamic force. It is a force like gravitation, and can travel or move in any area your thoughts focus on.
unknown

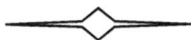

Electricity, Thoughts and Philosophy

Thoughts are giant-powers. They are more powerful than electricity. They control your life, mold your character, and shape your destiny. Mark how one thought expands into many thoughts, within a short time. Suppose you get an idea to set up a tea-party for your friends. The one thought of 'tea' invites instantaneously the thoughts of sugar, milk, tea-cups, tables, chairs, table-cloth, napkins, spoons, cakes, biscuits, etc. So, this world is nothing but the expansion of thoughts. The expansion of thoughts of the mind towards the objects is bondage; and, the renunciation of thoughts is liberation.
unknown

———◇———

Be observant in stopping past negative thoughts.

Spoken Phrases to Think About

Change your negative thoughts to whatever you want.

Thoughts take action.

What you're thinking is going to be the result of action.

Knowledge of your thoughts is important.

I read a book recently that said many people chase 'time' and then complain about not having enough time. When I read this statement it made me chuckle because it reminded me of how I experienced that myself.

I remember when I thought about publishing my book, acquiring more therapy sessions, painting, and designing a new garden, and of course I wanted to take some trips.

Guess what? All of those thoughts became reality. I did publish my book and started another and another and got calls for therapy sessions like I'd never gotten before. My painting became a fun thing and I kept painting with oils and someone gave me plants to re-design my garden, then the calls began; invitations for trips.

I moaned to myself that I didn't have enough time in a day to accomplish it all, and if I did it anyway, I was exhausted by the end of the day.

It was me in the first place that brought all of those things into my life; by my own thoughts.

Not too many years ago I felt stuck or imprisoned by my current circumstances. I moaned and complained a lot to myself and then one day, I remembered I had wanted that relationship. I had thought about it. I had asked for it. Guess what? I got it. My current reality at that time was a result of my thoughts I had been thinking. I see the light now. I am careful what I think about, what I daydream about, because I want to be sure it's what I want in my life and what I want to do with my life.

Thoughts are powerful.

———————◇———————

A friend of mine who is a medical doctor recently shared a story when I told him about the book I am writing.

He said, "Pattimari, I know from experience that nothing is *incurable*. I've seen patients with the same disease, same area; one would die from it, while another would not and become cured. I looked over my notes and discovered the ones that had been cured were the very ones who mentioned they believed they could be cured. In my mind, I'm convinced thoughts do have a lot to be considered when it comes to how we live our life and how we cure ourselves." He went on to tell me story after story about his patients that were cured. He said most had a positive spirit and not much seemed to disturb them because they believed in the cure. In one case, the two men; doctor and patient, became friends. My friend watched his patient soar out of sight and was intrigued by the patient's imagination and faith.

This same doctor scheduled a luncheon with his close friend who was also a medical doctor, and the three of us dipped into stories and how the power of thought works so miraculously. That same day he shared a story about a man who had been told he had cancer. The man immediately began meditating, eating healthy and convincing his mind to believe he would be cured. This doctor told me, he had to admit, he didn't think this would happen because his cancer was so far along, but in the end he said he had to change his thinking because the man was indeed cured a year later. He declared that he would never doubt another patient again.

There is abundance for *all* in this world to join this way of thinking and to make your life a better one with great happiness. Know that all good things are within you and available for you to use. It is yours. Test it. Change your thoughts today and see how your life will change.

Heal your thoughts

Meditation can change your negative thought~

Chapter Fifteen

Books read with inspiration

I recently read a book titled 'The Secret,' and became so inspired by it that I want to share some of it with you. The book is written by Rhonda Byrne.

When we look around us, even at our own bodies, what we see is the tip of the iceberg.
Dr. John Hagelin

Think of this for a moment. Look at your hand. It looks solid, but it's really not. If you put it under a proper microscope you'd see a mass of energy vibrating.
Bob Proctor

Everything is made up of the exact same thing, whether it's your hand, the ocean, or a star.
John Assaraf

Everything is energy, and let me help you to understand that just a little bit. There's the Universe, our galaxy, our planet, and then individuals, and then inside of this body are organ systems, then cells, then molecules, and the atoms. And then there is energy. So there are a lot of levels to think about, but everything in the Universe is energy.
Dr. Ben Johnson

In Rhonda Byrne's book Charles Hoanel says, "The Universal Mind is not only intelligence, but it is substance, and this substance is the attraction force which brings electrons together by the law of attraction so they form atoms; the atoms in turn are brought together by the same law and form molecules; molecules take objective forms and so we find that the law is the creative force behind every manifestation, not only of atoms, but of worlds, of the Universe, of everything of which the imagination can for any conception"

When I read these words, I pondered on them for a full hour and connected with the thought that we are all connected in this Universe. If you think that we can talk through little wires (telephone) across the entire world and not be connected mind to mind, then why is it that we can hear a voice through a little wire for thousands of miles away? I have to admit when I read a stimulating book, my mind soars with all sorts of thoughts, questions and insights.

Charles Hoanel talked about, in Rhonda Byrne's book, that to become conscious of this power is to become a 'live wire.' He went on to say, "The Universe is the live wire." Think about that...Does the Universe carry power to meet every situation in the life of every individual? When the individual mind touches the Universal Mind, does it receive all its power? I say it does. However, I wonder why all this has been a secret. Why hasn't the world connected to this? Do you think it would be in the state it is right now if we all connected to this secret? No, it wouldn't. I can't believe it would.

Many film makers, producers and writers have tried to clue us in, but it didn't sink in. I question why this is so. But there I go again, dreaming of a better world; a world of peace, instead of war and violence. I wonder if it would be possible to bring the entire world to peace if we all had thoughts of peace. I believe it could happen, that is, if we all became *One Universal Mind* working together.

Another part in the book says, "We are not our past."
All of you that had dark pasts; the ones with abusive parents or unhappy families that carried your thoughts into dark places where you felt like a victim can now change those unhappy thoughts. Recreate those thoughts. Make happy thoughts; Ones that will open doors for you and make your life a better life. We can and do have the power to change those dark thoughts. Those happenings are way back in our childhood and now we're here. We can become like a producer or actor and change our lines to different lines, or our pictures to different ones. We're safe now. We are no longer fearful children. We made it! We grew up and now we have the power to be who we want to be. Act like we want and be all the things we dream and think about. We can make our own realities!
We can make our own life! We can be happy! JoAnn, Charlotte and I have often discussed how wonderful it would be if the world connected and set our world in peaceful realities. It can happen, if we keep passing on the word until the whole world believes in the power of thought and changes our world realities.

This is someone who dreamed of being a published poet. This is his reality.

Somewhere Between the Pages and the Words I Fell in Love

I have been here before
Somewhere between the paper and the pen,
Between the sentences and the paragraphs,
Between the dotting of I's and the crossing of T's, between the cousins of the G and the Q.
Somewhere between the empty pages, words will start to appear and flow like a wonder in love with expressing the scribbles I compress upon this paper of a pad forgotten.
Now remembering with every loop and line what we fell in love with as a child; somewhere between the silver chair and Max the "Wild Thing King".
I fell in love with the words of others; somewhere between the numbers of fifteen and thirty-two; I found a frost upon the pages of an old poetry book.
Melting upon the tips of my fingers; outlining the very soul of my finger prints slowly drip, drip, and dripping down the side of my pen; roll, roll, and rolling across the paper and leisurely soaking into the pages of the binder that held my words that I loved so dear.
Somewhere between my thoughts, my heart, my mind and the child that has become the man I am today the passion has grown with me for the words of others who came before me.
To share my words somewhere between the pages; hoping someone will fall in love with the words I write as well.

© John McKinley Pride Jr

Chapter Sixteen

JoAnn's Soul Food for Depression

Years ago, I found myself in a deep, dark depression. A series of tragic circumstances plunged me into the deepest despair I'd ever known, and I could see no way out. I went to my therapist regularly, and took the temporary medication she recommended, but still I couldn't bring myself to feel any joy in life. All seemed so desperately hopeless and full of despair. I felt like I'd never be able to rise up from such a totally dark night.

Since the therapy and medication weren't helping very much, I decided to see if something else might help. Having been an avid reader all my life, I began to read books that claimed to offer help in overcoming dark feelings and depressions. I studied every book like this that I could find - books by sages and seers, books by philosophers and natural psychologists, books by people from all times and places who might be able to help me leave depression behind for good.

After some time spent studying these people, I began to realize that I had the inner resources to change my way of thinking, which led to a change in my way of feeling. Studying these teachings enabled me to see that I had the ability to be in charge of my thoughts and feelings, that depression was not something I had to endure in any way.

I was amazed to discover that all of these people (I call them soul doctors) agree in teaching that we are responsible for our thoughts and feelings and that we are obligated to live rationally and ethically, and that we must do so if we want to regain or maintain psychological health. These wise people knew past all controversy that there are clear and definite rules of mental health that must be practiced if we want to live happy, peaceful and healthy lives.

For years, I had nourished my heart on fantasies, on nightmares of anxiety, along with terribly negative feelings and thoughts, until after awhile these illusive fears and hatreds and angers seemed more real to me than Reality itself. By doing this habitually to myself, I had made myself sick in heart and soul. I became depressed because I had forgotten how Life really wants us to live.

Here at last, in the teachings of these true psychologists of the past and present, was the cure I sought for overcoming the darkness.

Who are these soul doctors? Beginning with Plato in the 5th century BC in ancient Greece, on up through the beginning years of Christianity with such people as Origen, Clement of Alexandria and St Augustine, the consensus is the same - we create the world we live in by the thoughts we choose to think. Eastern traditions have always taught these things too. The middle ages and the Renaissance saw an upsurge of this Truth in people such as Meister Eckhart, Hildegard of Bingen, Thomas aKempis and Emanuel Swedenborg, to mention just a few. Modern times also has its spokesmen for these Truths - Pierre Teilhard deChardin, Carl Jung, Matthew Fox, Joseph Campbell and many others carry on the Tradition of psychological Truth that was laid down in ancient times.

All of these soul doctors, plus many more which are quoted throughout this book, knew the Truth of our inner psycho/spiritual nature, and they have offered us the tools that we need to overcome depression and anxiety. Their voices are the collective Voice of our ancestors, the Voice of the World Consciousness, guiding and instructing us in how to live happily and peacefully, no matter what our outer situation in life may be. The Truth is there for all of us to see and feed upon, available in virtually every public library, and now also on the internet.

Every journey, no matter how long, begins with one small, simple step. We must begin to claim our birthright of healthy thinking by exchanging our negative thoughts for positive ones. If, throughout the day, we are assailed by a thousand negative, depressive thoughts, we must take each one and refuse to allow it to master our mood. Usually a depression contains one or two major thoughts that run around in our minds like squirrels in a cage. For instance, perhaps you find yourself constantly thinking, "I never do anything right." You must learn to change this erroneous thinking to its opposite - the Truth. The Truth is that you have done many, many things in your life that are right, and good, and beautiful, and now it is time, if you really want to end your depression, to think this truth - "I DO accomplish at least some things right!" We must say this to ourselves until we begin to really feel that Truth deep inside of us, until the negative lies we tell ourselves fade away into nothingness.

Or suppose you habitually think "Life is miserable. I wish I could end it all". When you think life is miserable, you are not thinking Truth. The world consensus, as well as the one harmonious voice of our soul doctors knows the opposite of this, that Life is precious, good, worth it. If we seek for the Truth, if we sincerely work towards re-recognizing the Truth of the innate goodness of Life, we will be enabled to open our eyes to see it.

These soul doctors are also unanimous in declaring that we must obey the Golden Rule at all times in every situation, treating others as we wish to be treated, looking outward to help others rather than brooding on our own inner ills. We must learn to love ourselves truly and deeply so that we can give this Love to others. Part of the cause of our depression lies in the fact that we pay too much attention to our own personal thoughts and feelings, becoming absorbed in our own musings and reactions to life, rather than looking outward and upward toward all that Life can be. We *are* Love. We *are* compassion. We *are* joy and hope and faith. We cheat ourselves and others when we refuse to recognize these facts.

Gratitude is an attitude that is completely forgotten while we're in a state of depression. Yet our soul doctors claim that gratitude for Life is always called for, always appropriate, always necessary in order to live depression-free. In every life, there are myriads of things we can be grateful for. I'm reminded yet again of the beauty of Helen Keller and her amazing power of vision into the true facts of life. Here was a woman deprived of the gifts of life that most of us take for granted - she was blind, deaf, and unable to talk. Yet she refused to be depressed. "Truly I have looked into the very heart of darkness" she exclaims, and we believe her, not being able to imagine such a terribly challenged life, "Truly I have looked into the very heart of darkness and yet I refused to yield to its paralyzing influence. I use my will, choose life and reject its opposite, nothingness." The next time you find yourself complaining about your life circumstances, feeling somehow cheated and filled with self-pity, take a look again at these brightly lit words of Helen and know that you do indeed have much to be grateful for, and get busy on concentrating on these gifts. If you do, you'll see a new world open up before (and behind!) your eyes.

Selfishness is a breeding ground for mental disorders of all kinds, our soul doctors tell us. Every spiritual tradition says that we reap what we sow, and this is as true of our inner dynamics as it is in the outer world. Charles Leadbeater, a contemporary esotericist, says in his book 'The Inner Life' "It is because we are the center of our own circle that we are liable to depression, for that comes only to one who is thinking of himself." And Alice Bailey, another contemporary student of our inner nature, says it even more clearly in her book 'Discipleship in the New Age', "Depression is a synonym for selfishness." Reach out to others who are in need of help; plan to make someone's day just a little better because of you. If you don't have the means of physical help, you can always pray and meditate for others, seeing them whole and happy. Your thoughts will do more than you realize to help others, and such good thoughts will also help you in your own cure.

If we are honest with ourselves, we must admit that the above truths are an integral part of our inner Being. They are the blueprints which compose our psycho/spiritual nature. We knew this instinctively as children, and we can know it once again as we practice these prescriptions for mental and emotional health. We must choose to live as ethically aware and responsible human beings. We must begin to change the habits of thought which we have allowed to crowd our minds to the exclusion of all truth. We must take control of our attitude towards life and refuse to give the negative a voice and place in our minds and hearts. Once we do, a whole new world will open up for us.

Here's a further sampling of why and how we must think the really true thoughts if we want to cure ourselves of depression;

Waste no time in self-pity or self-justification. Know the law has placed you where you are, and where you best can serve,

and learn that difficulties are ever of a man's own making and the result of his own mental attitude.
 Alice A Bailey - A Treatise On White Magic

Let each one of us dig down after the root of darkness which is within us, and let us pluck it out of our hearts from the root. It will be plucked out if we recognize it. But if we are ignorant of it, it takes root in us and produces its fruits in our hearts. It masters us. We are its slaves. It is powerful because we have not recognized it. The Gospel of Philip

The world in which a man lives shapes itself chiefly by the way in which he looks at it." Arthur Schopenhauer
"Human beings, by changing the inner attitudes of their minds, can change the outer aspects of their lives.
 William James, American Psychologist

If you be sick, your own thoughts make you sick.
Ben Johnson, English dramatist +1637

If you are distressed by anything external, the pain is not due to the thing itself, but to your estimate of it; and thus you have the power to revoke it at any minute.
Marcus Aurelius, Roman Emperor and Philosopher

Change your thoughts and you change the world.
Norman Vincent Peale, American clergyman and author

The Journey Within

The sages born in every age send forth their heartfelt plea
"Look deep within and know yourself and then you will be free;
Give up all cares and burdens; find the Center deep inside;
Shed the sheath of outworn concepts. Know yourself!" the seers cried.
So I took the inner journey, traveled worlds within my mind,
Armed with trustful, open searching, I sought all that I could find;
Down to seas of cells becoming, up to realms of birthing stars,
Webs of crystallized emotions forming painful inner wars.
With a thrusting trust I sort through all the psychic webs I've made,
All the hatreds and the jealousies, the dreams I left to fade,
The times I hurt my brothers and the times I hurt my pride,
The times of hollow laughter when I really should have cried.
These webbings halt my journey to below and to above,
They will not stop their screaming till I see that they need Love.
So I listen very softly to the sadness they portray -
Acceptance brings the Light I need to find my Centered Way.
So I made the inner journey, and imagine my surprise!

The shadow feelings dissipate; I see through all their lies!
And the fruit of this sweet travel to below and to above
Is to see the Truth quite clearly - I am never-ending Love.

Change your thoughts today~

Chapter Seventeen

Charlotte's Story of Changing our Thoughts

Growing up as a little girl Jackie had low self esteem. Some could say it was because her father was an alcoholic and a womanizer, which left her mother being the father and mother of the household. Needless to say, she didn't get a lot of love from her father; never getting a hug or kiss or even one word of love.

However, even though he wasn't around much, his children loved him and they knew he loved them. But for a little girl that still wasn't enough, so consequently while growing up she didn't like who she was. She often said and knew she didn't have a bad childhood, but many times didn't think anyone cared.

She was the middle child so she had to compromise more than the other siblings; always feeling *herself worth* was zero. Yes, you guessed it - Jackie chose abusive husbands that were alcoholics and womanizers just like her father. She continued searching for someone to love her. During her second divorce, she met a friend who taught her how to meditate. And that changed her life forever!

While going through her second divorce her mind was spinning with feelings of guilt, depression, anger, fear, shame, sadness and loneliness. She thought she was a failure and would fail again, so consequently she was totally at war with herself; always punishing herself and not forgiving her mistakes *she thought* she had made. The greatest fear she had was the possibility of destroying a good relationships that might come her way.

She discovered one day, through meditation that she had imagined all these things in her mind and decided to let go of her *dark past thoughts* and make new ones. So she went to work on developing new paintings of herself; turning the past thoughts into new thoughts.

In order to remove the clutter which was painful and left her feeling lonely, she turned to meditation to slay the dragons and build new cleansing thoughts. After several weeks of meditation, she finally made peace with herself. Each morning she looked at her reflection in the mirror and began to say affirmations.

I love who I am I love me
I love that person in the mirror
I am a good person
People do love me
I deserve to be happy
I love and give out love
I am loved

Soon after repeating these affirmations each morning, she started feeling better about herself. She was at peace. She changed past thoughts into new thoughts. It worked!

Today, she is a happy person who experiences joy and soon after waking up each morning she is full of excitement, energy and looks forward to her new day.
Thoughts are powerful. Love is powerful.

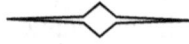

Think about these phrases

If we believe life is a struggle, it will be a struggle. What we think creates our reality.

Jackie stopped thinking she was a failure who didn't deserve love and her life became blissful.

Every thought we think, every word we say - is an affirmation! Our thoughts are affirming subconsciously what direction our life will go in.

By having negative thoughts we create negative action - to be stored as tension in the body, but by using positive affirmations, thoughts and positive techniques *it is possible* to achieve anything you want. It transforms you; your health, a renewed joy, and a passion for life that sends you out smiling every day.

Repeating positive affirmations for a few minutes and then thinking negatively the rest of the day, neutralizes the effects of the positive words. You have to refuse thinking negative thoughts, if you wish to attain positive results.

Positive Affirmations

I am surrounded by love
My mind is calm
I have a lot of energy
People around me, love me

Wealth is coming to me
I am happy
I am filled with Joy
I am at peace with my life
I love who I am
I am calm and relaxed in every situation
My thoughts are under my control
I radiate love and happiness wherever I go
My body is healthy and it gets better every day
I love my body
I am successful in whatever I do
Everything is getting better every day
Every cell in my body vibrates energy and good health
I know now that I deserve love and accept it
I rejoice in the love I encounter everyday
When I believe in myself, so do others
I am my own unique self, special, creative and wonderful.
My life is a joy filled with love, fun, and friendship
I choose Joy, love, peace
I open my heart and allow amazing things to flow into my life
I am not a failure.

If we use these positive words in our daily lives, we will be changed forever and we will be creating a happy blissful life! Not just for ourselves, but for others around us. What we put out comes back, and if it's all positive it will come back positive. If we all create a positive environment it will become contagious and spread though-out our planet. Open your heat and let it shine. Shine your light!

How Thoughts Can Change People

Positive Thinking by Choice

My husband, Ronald G. Huston, PhD., and I ran fifteen residential treatment facilities together, a non-profit high school and a treatment clinic for at risk adolescent youth for almost twenty years. I remember one particular young man who I became very fond of; I will call him Isaac to protect his identity.

It was late one summer and I had just finished teaching a life skills class to some of the boys, when a staff member approached me and said that Isaac had not been working his program and was acting out for the last few weeks. She was concerned, as I was, because this was out of the ordinary for Isaac.

The next day, after school, I pulled him aside and talked with him about his behavior. He was aloof and withdrawn; before I could get to the core of his problem we exchanged our own stories which many times brought us both to tears. Here is this kid who is rather large in stature and disguised as a tough guy breaking down like a little boy who just feel off his bike and skinned his knees. He spoke mostly about his hardships while growing up in a poor family in a run-down city belonging to a major gang.

By the end of our discussion and stories, I realized, Isaac was terrified of going home and getting back into the same situation he was before he came to us. He feared returning to his same dysfunctional family would lead him back into trouble again.

I told him to look at this as a positive change in his life and that it would be up to him to keep his thoughts directed in a positive way. Otherwise it would be his choice to make it a positive 'returning home' by using positive thoughts. I gave Isaac a plan and here is the plan I gave him.

1. Use positive thinking to realize your own potential

2. Ask yourself what can I do to make a difference; to make positive changes in my life?

3. What can I do to help others make positive changes in their life?

4. Setting realistic goals using positive thinking.

5. Putting your plan into action.

I told Isaac that he was a positive influence on some of the other boys when he wasn't getting wrapped up in all of the negative thoughts, which made him fearful. I saw first- hand that he took these boys under his wing to help them run a smooth program. Isaac was a leader and didn't even know that himself. I told him that his positive thoughts were leading him in the right direction.

Isaac graduated from his program a few weeks later and went home. I got a phone call from his mother after a short period and she was so thrilled to tell me that Isaac had a positive-attitude helping out around the house. She continued to tell me that one afternoon she saw Isaac sitting on a broken down block wall with some of his old friends in his gang; he was teaching them the program that he had learned in the group home. I knew then that Isaac realized his own potential and that he would be all right because he had changed his fearful negative thoughts to positive thoughts.

Linda M. Huston, M.A., C.F.L.E. (Certified Family Life Educator

Billy was referred by the Probation Department to our group home because he was getting into fights at school and with his siblings. Billy was so angry that when he shouted at his parents and police they became afraid of him. Immediately when he entered the group home he had everyone on edge.

Billy started verbal confrontations that eventually led to fist fights with the staff, residents and even tried to start a fight with me, his therapist. We had consequences in the group home for fighting which resulted in a loss of privileges. After a while Billy got tired of not having privileges so he started going to therapy sessions and slowly began to open up with his feelings. He said he was angry all the time because he was modeling his father who was an angry man and was abusive with his mother. His words were; " I feel mad a lot, once in awhile happy, but depressed a lot."

I explained to Billy that we act according to how we are feeling at the time.

I worked with Billy to help him identify and learn to recognize other emotions he was feeling; frustrate, joy, annoyed, excited, peaceful, and love. When he started to get angry, I asked him to really look at what emotion he was feeling at the time. As time went on Billy's emotional vocabulary became bigger and he began to label what he was feeling.

Billy began showing positive interactions and admitted he had always felt more in control when he was angry. He saw right away he paid a big price for that angry feeling and changed his thoughts to concentrate on working hard to not get angry.

In a few months Billy was not the same person who had come to the group home. He made friends among the staff and residents, as well as, school.

Just by Billy changing his thoughts he made a better life for himself. He graduated and continues to do well. He learned from therapy sessions in the group home to pay attention to what he was really feeling before he reacted. He now wants to help young people with their anger problems before it ruins their life like it almost did his before he changed his thoughts to more positive thoughts.

Ronald G. Huston, PhD, MSW, MPH, Licensed Clinical Psychologist

Words from Linda and Ronald Huston – "We have many more stories to tell, but it will be in Pattimari and Charlotte's next book."

Chapter Eighteen

A Women's Group Story and More

A few months ago, I started a therapy group with five women who claimed all they wanted was to be free of their anger and be happy. One stated all she wanted was to rid herself of all her fears that keep her awake at night.

On that first session, I said, "Okay group, this seems simple enough to accomplish, but I can't take away your anger, make you happy, or rid you of your fears."
Before I could go farther in my explanation one of the women said, "Well, I suppose I better get up and go home and drown myself. I'm angry enough to get angry at you for having me pay my fee and then tell me you can't help me. It hardly seems to be worth our going on."
I chuckled and said, "It *is* worth going on because what I'm going to tell and show you will change your life forever."
"Oh," said one of women, "Really, I wasn't trying to be rude. I was just trying to demonstrate my problem with anger." Every one of us laughed and this group of women became excited about the message I was going to give them.

I asked them if they were aware of what they think about or when their fear, anger and so on occurs. A couple of the women nodded no, while the other three stated they did know.
I said, "Okay, let me share something with you about your thoughts and how amazing *thought power* is because you can literally think things into existence and make it a reality right now. One of the women set up straight and said, "This sounds

crazy, but somehow, I think you're going to show us it isn't crazy at all."

I smiled and said, "It isn't crazy at all. In fact science has proven that everything starts from the mind. Your reality expands as you think and is shaped by that draft you form in your thoughts. Ancient religions knew this. Whether you believe it or not, your thoughts become your reality." I went on to say that they could manifest the annulment of fear, or to rid themselves of anger.

Just before the group session ended I sent them home with homework. First of all, I requested they begin to be aware of their thoughts and to jot them down faithfully and compare their fears and anger to what their thoughts were shortly before they felt these emotions. Secondly, I asked them to start training their thoughts to have positive thoughts - where they'd think about good things happening rather than fearful things. Lastly, I asked the women who had anger issues to write down every time they felt angry and bring it to the group the following week, but to immediately smile or laugh each time they felt angry. One woman asked me how she could laugh or smile when she was feeling angry. I chuckled and said, "That exactly the point, because you can't feel both at the same time."
"Oh, she said, "then it would turn my anger into happiness?" I said, "Yes."

You see, every living human being is constantly in the state of expression, growing and building their life upon what they think, but many never realize this. For example, the science of quantum physics has already proven that the center of everything is energy, *including our thoughts*. So when you exercise power over your thoughts, you are actually starting to create your reality - ***deliberately***. In reality, you are shaping them with a goal in mind.

The power of the thought creates feelings and emotions that you have when you think that thought.

Now, let's think a little deeper and see if I can paint you a painting of what I'm trying to convey to you. Powerful positive emotion is none other than gratitude. Why? Well, because when you appreciate something, you are actually activating the *law of attraction* by using it to create **more** instead of less. (Law of attraction is simply things you attract to your life by your thoughts.) For example, if you desire something and believe it, the energies in the Universe attaches itself to you. It's almost works like a magnet. There's nothing magical about it - it's just the way it works.

You are in reality, channeling your energy toward it becoming a reality. Energy streams where attention goes.

Dr. Wayne Dyer once said, "Abundance is something that we tune into."

The Universe responds to thoughts, whether it be good or bad. So let it stream freely.

Donald Trump's wealth awareness is as high as the sky. He attracts money and admits it.

To conclude this thought, be careful of what you think. Be aware of your thoughts. If you doubt it happens this way, keep a journal, watch your thought process and test it. Try it!

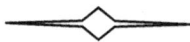

———◇———

Words of Wisdom

Life is a game
What you get out of it
Depends on
How you plan

Desire is the software of the soul

How you look at something
Is what you will see

Keep your thoughts
Happy
So you will be happy

How you think is important

Part II of this book will be coming out soon

Pattimari Sheets-Diamond, Charlotte Huston-Johnson, JoAnn Kite

Sometimes your Greatest Misery is your Greatest Happiness

9 780557 426331